Elizabethan
Shakespeare

Elizabethan Shakespeare

Peter Milward, S.J.

Sapientia Press
of Ave Maria University

Sapientia Press
of Ave Maria University
5050 Ave Maria Blvd.
Ave Maria, FL 34142
888-343-8607

Cover Design: Eloise Anagnost

Cover Images: Portrait of Queen Elizabeth I (1533–1603)
(panel) by Nicholas Hilliard (1547–1619) (manner of)
© Philip Mould Ltd., London/The Bridgeman Art Library

G.11631.B.L. Title Page with a Portrait of Shakespeare, from
Mr William Shakespeare's Comedies, Histories and Tragedies, edited
by J. Heminge and H. Condell, engraving by Droeshout, 1623
© British Library, London, UK/© British Library Board.
All Rights Reserved/The Bridgeman Art Library

Printed in the United States of America.

Library of Congress Control Number: 2007940921

ISBN: 978-1-932589-47-4

Table of Contents

chapter 1

Introducing
William Shakespeare

▓ The Man

I T IS STRANGE how few people—even Shakespeare scholars—think of asking the most obvious questions about William Shakespeare! I mean, for example, a question such as, "Who is Shakespeare?" Of those who do ask that question, most have the wrong idea in mind. They imagine that the plays and poems that have come down to us under the name of "Shakespeare" may have been written by someone else—maybe Sir Francis Bacon, or Christopher Marlowe, or the Earl of Oxford, or Queen Elizabeth. But what they are really asking is not, "Who is Shakespeare?" in the present, but, "Who was Shakespeare?" in the past. So most scholars relegate these questioners to "the lunatic fringe," and they will have nothing more to do with them. The question becomes, in other words, out of the question.

No, I am not thinking about such theories. I am content to take Shakespeare as he is in the present, with his plays and poems—however dubious may be the attribution of some of them. I am even content with the myths and legends that have grown up around his name. However, I cannot be content with his mere name, or anything connected with his name, except as a starting point for exploration. In fact, for my starting point I propose to take some words he dared to utter in one of his sonnets, "I am that I am" (cxxi). Why "dared"? Cannot anyone say the same thing of himself? Yes, but we have to remember who it was that first made that statement about himself. When Moses dared to ask God, "What is your name?" God dared to answer, "I am that I am" (Exod iii.14). Here we may well admire the condescension of God, in deigning (or daring) to place himself on a level not just with angels and human beings, but with all existing beings. It is as if God wishes in speaking with Moses to emphasize what he has in common with all beings. That is, simply, that he "is," or preferably in the first person singular, "I am," or rather in capital letters, "I AM." After all, other beings, as creatures, have to qualify their existence with some addition to differentiate themselves. They have to add a complement to the verb "to be," and they have to use small letters as a token of their essential humility. But only God can say of himself, "I AM." Only God is what he is, in the literal sense of the words. Yet on others, especially on rational beings, he confers the privilege of echoing him. That is what Shakespeare recognizes in this sonnet. On the other hand, with Shakespeare, as with other men and other created beings, we have to add the opposite statement—as the dramatist does through the voices of Viola in *Twelfth Night* (iii.1) and Iago in *Othello* (i.1)—"I am not what I am." How paradoxical, yet how true! Shakespeare is at once himself and not himself. He both is and is not. He attracts us to himself in all his plays and poems, and at the same time he repels us. There is a mystery both in himself and in them. It is an essential characteristic of mystery that it is at once fascinating and terrifying. So when we approach him, fascinated by the enigma of his personality, he seems to warn us, as Hamlet warned his schoolmates

Rosencrantz and Guildenstern, not to "pluck out the heart of my mystery" (*Hamlet* iii.2).

I can't help doing this at the beginning of this book on Shakespeare. I can't help beginning with the question that is most basic to his being, namely, the question put by the caterpillar to Alice at the beginning of her adventures in wonderland, "Who are you?" The first thing one has to realize about so great a genius as Shakespeare, and to a lesser extent about ourselves, is that he is who he is. He inhabits (as G. K. Chesterton would say) a wonderland of his own, and with his poems and plays he invites us to enter that wonderland, partly for our entertainment, partly for our instruction. Everything he has written, and everyone who appears in his writings, is wonderful, an inhabitant of his wonderland. This is what he shows us above all through the innocent eyes of his last heroine, Miranda, when she exclaims at the end of his last play, *The Tempest*, "O wonder! / How many goodly creatures are there here! / How beauteous mankind is! O brave new world, / That has such creatures in it!" (v.1). Then we have to add that Shakespeare not only is and is not, not only a created being—partly like God, partly like all that is not God—but also in particular a human being. This, too, has to be emphasized from the outset, that Shakespeare is human. For it is only too easy to fall into the trap, laid by so many well-meaning Romantics and Victorians, of imagining Shakespeare as a superman, as a Herculean hero, as a god. No! He is what he is. He is not the Supreme Being, nor even a perfect human being, but an imperfect, weak, sinful human being, subject to the same errors as we all are. As he himself insists with reference to Henry V in speaking with his soldiers on the eve of Agincourt: "The king is but a man as I am. The violet smells to him as it doth to me. The element shows to him as it doth to me. All his senses have but human conditions. His ceremonies laid by, in his nakedness he appears but a man" (*Henry V* iv.1). In other words, into his mouth we may well put the motto of the Roman dramatist Terence, *"Homo sum. Humani nil a me alienum puto."* (I am a man. Nothing human I regard as foreign to me.) But then, being a man, Shakespeare (it must be emphasized) is neither universal nor infinite, for all the protests of his idolaters to the contrary. He was not what his friend and rival Ben Jonson said of him, "not of an age, but for all time." Certainly, he has already proved the extent to which he may be said to belong to all ages, even the extent of four centuries and the ends of the earth, wherever the English language is used and understood. But he was definitely a man of his own age, first Elizabethan and then Jacobean. Nor was he, in the words of a famous song, "a Russian, a French or Turk or Prussian, or perhaps Italian," but "an Englishman." In this respect (though not in other respects), I warmly applaud what George Bernard Shaw has said about Shakespeare, as well as about himself: "The man who writes about himself and his own time is the only man who writes about all people and about all time" (*The Sanity of Art*, 1908).

■ The Englishman

Now at last let me come down from the clouds of ontology and anthropology to the place and time where William Shakespeare first came into existence, if, in the words of another William, "trailing clouds of glory /From God who is our home" (William Wordsworth, "Immortality Ode"). The place was Stratford-upon-Avon (or more simply, Stratford) in the county of Warwickshire, in the heart of the English Midlands. The time was the month of April 1564, some five or six years after the accession of Queen Elizabeth, leaving the first thirty-nine years of Shakespeare's life to be spent in the Elizabethan age. We know the precise date of his baptism, April 26, 1564, as well as the precise date of his death, April 23, 1616, and so we like to think he was also born on that day, which happens to be the feast-day of England's patron saint, St. George.

Neither of Shakespeare's parents, John Shakespeare or Mary Arden, were native to Stratford; they only came to settle there, one after the other, in the late 1550s. It is rather in the neighboring Forest of Arden that we have to look for the families of both Arden and Shakespeare. This may indicate that the young William wasn't just the "country boy of Stratford," as imagined by anti-Stratfordians. Rather, he might well be called a complete country bumpkin, if not a forester. He might even be regarded, as he was by the French of the "Enlightenment" period, as a barbarian. Still, if I use these words about him, I mean them in no pejorative sense, but with approval—as when John Milton spoke of him (in *L'Allegro*) as "Sweetest Shakespeare, Fancy's child," warbling "his native woodnotes wild." In other words, as his plays attest, Shakespeare was a countryman, close to nature and close to Mother Earth. As Friar Laurence, one of Shakespeare's many mouthpieces, says: "The Earth that's Nature's mother is her tomb. / What is her burying grave, that is her womb" (*Romeo and Juliet*, ii.3).

On the other hand, I must add, Shakespeare was more than a countryman, however close to nature and the earth he shows himself to be, not least of all in *As You Like It* with its setting in the Forest of Arden. What wasn't always realized by critics, such as Ben Jonson and John Milton, who emphasized his natural genius is that in Shakespeare's case nature and tradition go hand in hand. Revolution may be hatched in cities, with their addiction to newfangled ways, but tradition is highly prized in the countryside. In another of his sonnets, Shakespeare contrasts the "new-found methods" and "compounds strange" of modern city poets with his own tendency to write "all one, ever the same" and to "keep invention in a noted weed" (lxxvi)—as if making his own the motto of which Queen Elizabeth boasted with less justification, *"Semper idem."*

The Catholic

The difference between these two ideals of nature and tradition may be put quite simply. For Shakespeare, nature was pagan, as we see in the fairies under Oberon and Titania (another name for Diana) of *A Midsummer Night's Dream*, and tradition was Catholic. Here we touch upon an even more basic aspect of the dramatist's genius, one that has been glossed over by Shakespearian critics from the time of those mentioned above. We also touch upon the tragedy of the age in which he lived, a tragedy that entered deeply into his dramatic genius as well, namely, that of the Reformation. It might be said that without the Reformation we would have had no Shakespeare. He was what he was because of the religious changes that were taking place all around him, from the time of his birth, even in so seemingly remote a county as Warwickshire. Not that he agreed with those changes, for then he would not have become so great a dramatist; rather he deeply disagreed with them, for, as I have said, he was a countryman in favor of tradition. For him that tradition, common to England and Europe, was Catholic, going back to the origins of both England and Europe and beyond them to the origins of Christianity. In his eyes, however, the new Protestants, who had come to power under the auspices of the so-called Virgin Queen, were revolutionaries from the cities and were engaged in destroying everything he held dear.

Yet from his point of view, and especially from the dramatic point of view he was to make his own, this new situation, however humanly unjust and even repellent it came to appear, was all to his advantage. With the newfangled bias imposed by the queen in favor of secularity—for it wasn't so much a Protestant church as a secular state that now came to prevail over England—Shakespeare may not have been free to express in his plays all he may have wished to express. Indeed, the cry of Hamlet, "But break, my heart, for I must hold my tongue!" (*Hamlet* i.2), is surely an echo of the dramatist's own deepest feelings. But in all his plays, he is striving to give expression to that which he cannot openly express, and that is what makes them so enigmatic, so fascinating, so Mona Lisa–esque. And that is what imparts to his mature drama the additional quality, all too rarely noticed by Shakespeare scholars, of "metadrama," or an unseen drama beyond that which we see on the stage.

To return to Shakespeare's native Warwickshire, it must not be thought, as some scholars still seem to be capable of thinking, that England changed overnight from a largely Catholic country under Queen Mary to a largely Protestant country under Queen Elizabeth in the year 1558. Warwickshire was particularly slow to accept the changes, as we may find in the laments uttered by the new bishop of Worcester, Edwin Sandys, well into the new reign. After ten years, he complains, "I have here long laboured to gain good will. The fruits of my travail are counterfeited countenances and hollow hearts." Men mostly accepted the changes only insofar as they were imposed from above, against their wishes, and they waited for yet another change, depending on the uncertain health of the Tudor queen and the likelihood of a Catholic succession under a Stuart queen.

The county was, however, divided between two dioceses, that of Worcester to the west, to which Stratford and the Forest of Arden belonged, and that of Coventry to the east. If Worcester was less willing to conform to the new changes, Coventry was more so, coming as it did under the powerful influence of the two Dudley brothers, Ambrose and Robert, respectively earls of Warwick and Leicester (at nearby Kenilworth). So within the Midland county of Warwickshire we encounter the religious division that was already coming to rend the country apart, with the old Catholics to the west and the new Protestants to the east. The west was, moreover, partly covered by the old Forest of Arden, with fond memories for the Shakespeares and the Ardens, while to the east lay the cities of the plain, Warwick and Coventry, with the castles of the two Protestant earls (both newly created earls by the new queen in 1561 and 1564). As for Robert Dudley, though his earldom was of Leicester, his castle of Kenilworth lay in Warwickshire, within easy reach of his brother's castle of Warwick. Of the two brothers he was the more powerful, since he was the queen's lover. What was more, like Ahab, the old king of Israel who had cast covetous eyes on Naboth's vineyard, he envied the real power of the head of the Arden family, Edward Arden of Parkhall—till he managed to bring his rival to an untimely end in the Tower of London in 1583. It may have been thanks to his father John, by then a prominent tradesman (a glover) in Stratford, that the young William could claim to be a real countryman. In any case, the country was never far from such a small town as Stratford. Yet it was through his mother, who hailed from a prosperous farming family in nearby Wilmcote, that he could trace his line of descent from the noblest in Warwickshire back to Saxon times as lords of Arden. It is in the light of this descent that we may understand one of the dramatist's deepest motives, bound up as he was through his family with both the religion and the tradition of England. This was a motive that must have inclined him to regard not only the Dudley brothers but also the Tudor rulers (being Welsh) as upstarts. Here we have the political situation implied in such plays of his as *As You Like It*, *Hamlet*, *Macbeth*, and *The Tempest*. Like Hamlet, the young Shakespeare was definitely not in favor of the new order in England. Rather, he would have agreed with Hamlet's friend Marcellus that "Something is rotten in the state" of England (*Hamlet* i.4).

The Tutor-Player

Such was the situation of Stratford at the time when the young William presumably began his schooling at the grammar school there—though we have no documentary evidence of his education whether at grammar school or at university. The school was barely five minutes' walk from his home in Henley Street, and it is interesting to note the identities of his schoolmasters during his presumed time there. What is of special interest is that they were all graduates of Oxford University, and most of them came from Lancashire—both places, especially the latter, hotbeds of what the Protestants came to term "Popery." It is also interesting to note how many of them had personal contacts with the newly founded Society of Jesus. One teacher, Simon Hunt, gave up his position as schoolmaster in 1575, taking a pupil, Robert Dibdale of Shottery, with him to the Catholic seminary at Douai (in the French Ardennes) before going on to join the Jesuits in Rome. Another, Thomas Jenkins, had been a fellow of St. John's College, Oxford, with the famous Edmund Campion before the latter went to Rome to enter the Society of Jesus. Yet a third, John Cottam, was brother to Thomas Cottam, who, after being ordained as a seminary priest, accompanied Campion to England in 1580 and was arraigned with Campion at Westminster Hall in 1581 before his own execution as a "traitor" (and a Jesuit) in 1582.

This Cottam was, moreover, the neighbor of a leading Catholic recusant gentleman in Lancashire, Alexander Houghton of Lea Hall near Preston. It may have been Cottam who recommended the young William, then aged fifteen, to Houghton. We know that Houghton kept tutors in his household, as did other Catholic gentlemen of the country, though it was against the law for them to do so. There is also a tradition, going back to the time when Shakespeare was dramatist for the Chamberlain's Men, that "he was a schoolmaster in the country." Then there is the mention of one "William Shakeshafte," as a promising young man connected with music and plays, in Houghton's will drawn up in August 1581, shortly before the testator's death. Again, it may be remembered that there was some fluidity in the form and spelling of Shakespeare's name, so that on moving to Lancashire he may well have assumed the form more familiar to the people in the Preston area. It may also be noted that when he did eventually come up to London, in the first printed allusion to him, in Robert Greene's *Groatsworth of Wit* (1592), he is ridiculed as "Shake-scene."

To return to Edmund Campion, it is fascinating to note how Campion's path seems to have intertwined with that of the young Shakespeare. William Allen, the founder of the Catholic seminary at Douai, had apparently served as usher at Stratford Grammar School about the year 1564 (the year of Shakespeare's birth), when he would have been known to John Shakespeare, who was one of the aldermen on the town council. Simon Hunt, after making his way from Stratford to Rome in 1575, would surely have met Campion there before the latter's journey to England in 1580, as being (with Persons) one of the few English Jesuits in Rome. Thomas Jenkins, too, would surely have had stories to tell his pupils at Stratford about memories of Campion at Oxford. Moreover, soon after his arrival in England we know that Campion was a guest of Sir William Catesby at Lapworth in the Forest of Arden, within a ten-mile ride by horse from Stratford. There John and William could not only have met the Jesuit, who might well have been informed of them before his coming, but also received from him the copy of that "Spiritual Testament" (formulated by St. Charles Borromeo and obtained from him at Milan) that was subsequently found hidden among the rafters of the house at Henley Street. Its authenticity provides us with a main piece of evidence that John Shakespeare intended to live and die as a loyal Catholic. Above all, if and when the young William made his way to Lancashire, no doubt with a letter of introduction from John Cottam, he would surely have renewed his acquaintance with Campion, who, we know, spent the spring of 1581 under the auspices of the Houghton family, whether with Alexander himself or his half-brother Richard.

With all this information about the young Shakespeare that has only recently come to light, we may well understand how it was that, while being a "country boy from Stratford," he was exposed from his earliest years to all the influences both in England and abroad that went into the making of what we call "Elizabethan England" or "early modern England." From Stratford to the area of Preston in mid-Lancashire he may seem to have been moving into the most backward of cultural backwaters, far from the center of the queen's court at Westminster, not to mention the universities of Oxford and Cambridge. Yet all this time he was hobnobbing not only with Oxford graduates at his grammar school but also with various Jesuits and Catholic gentlemen—in Warwickshire through the family of his Arden mother, and in Lancashire with the families first of Houghton, then of Hesketh, and finally of the Earl of Derby. This leads to Shakespeare's first known connection with the players called "Strange's Men," patronized by the son and heir of the Earl of Derby. The players performed not only at Derby's seat in Knowsley, Lancashire, but also in Stratford and London. This may all be theory, but it is a very plausible one, filling a gap in what has hitherto been a case of biographical ignorance.

Meanwhile, just a year after the suspiciously coinciding deaths of Campion and Houghton in 1581, we follow the young Shakespeare back to Stratford, whereupon he marries Anne Hathaway. We have no record of their wedding, only a formal application for the celebration of a wedding without banns during the season of Advent in 1582, at the diocesan registry office of Worcester, where the bride is mentioned as being not of Shottery (generally regarded as her home) but of Temple Grafton. Now, if Shakespeare was a Catholic, as all the evidence from Stratford and Lancashire suggests, he would have wished to celebrate the wedding with a Catholic ceremony. We also know that at this time the priest at Temple Grafton was an old Catholic priest from Marian times (referring to Queen Mary I) who had been allowed to remain at his church undisturbed, one Sir John Frith. Such a ceremony would not, however, have been recognized by the new Anglican Church, and so, after it had been performed by way of a "precontract," William and Anne would have had to get it officially recorded at the diocesan registry office of Worcester. This may also be a matter of theory, but it is interestingly echoed in two of Shakespeare's plays—in *As You Like It*, where Touchstone says of the Forest of Arden (on whose outskirts Temple Grafton is located), "Here we have no temple but the wood" (iii.3), and in *Measure for Measure*, where the lovers Claudio and Juliet are arrested on a charge of fornication, though they are engaged to each other by "precontract." In this way Shakespeare's elder daughter Susanna, who was born in May 1583, within six months of the supposed marriage of William and Anne, might well have been born (from a Catholic viewpoint) in holy wedlock.

This leads us to the beginning of Shakespeare's dramatic career, already in Lancashire, where he may have passed from Alexander Houghton's household, by way of Rufford Hall under Sir Thomas Hesketh (who is mentioned in Houghton's will as a likely successor), to Lord Strange's Men at Knowsley in Lancashire and so to London. It wasn't long after Shakespeare's arrival in London that the young dramatist drew down on himself the professional jealousy of Robert Greene (as author of *The Groatsworth of Wit*) and Christopher Marlowe (to whom *The Groatsworth of Wit* is addressed) for being "an upstart crow, beautified with our feathers" and "in his own conceit the only Shake-scene in a country." From then onward, however, we may turn our eyes from the foregoing biographical theories (however well substantiated) to the plays, concerning which Ben Jonson wrote in verses prefixed to the posthumously published First Folio of 1623, "Thou art a monument without a tomb, / And art alive still, while thy book doth live." It is of these plays that we may ask, What do they tell us about the inner heart of the dramatist?

chapter 2
Apprentice in History

Henry VI

FROM THE OUTSET of his dramatic career Shakespeare stands out as a historian, with no fewer than ten plays of English history to his credit, arranged in chronological order of kings, according to the First Folio of 1623, between the comedies and the tragedies. These plays, however, are hardly among his most memorable, and few lovers of Shakespeare would include even one of them among "the top ten." Yet some of them, notably *Richard III* and the Falstaff plays of *Henry IV*, won popularity at the time, which they have retained ever since. It may be asked why the dramatist devoted so much of his time to them when his genius lay rather in the fields of comedy and tragedy—though "history" is hardly a dramatic genre and, while *Richard III* is as much of a tragedy as *Macbeth*, the two parts of *Henry IV* with Falstaff in them are rather to be classed as comedies. Shakespeare's addiction to history may be traced partly to his love of England and his desire to communicate that love to members of his audience and partly to the evident popularity of the genre among the Englishmen of his day.

The first of these two reasons, Shakespeare's love of England, appears in the plays themselves, though it doesn't come to a climax till the later play of *Richard II* (called a "tragedy" in its original title). Here the dramatist, through the mouthpiece of the aged John of Gaunt, uncle to the wayward King Richard, seems to speak like "a prophet new inspir'd" in a long speech of some twenty lines characterized by the fond repetition of "this England" (ii.1). One might say that Shakespeare speaks not only as a prophet, looking forward through the eyes of Gaunt to the impending troubles England was to face during the Wars of the Roses, but also as a patriot. Only his patriotism is as far from the jingoist's defense of "my country, right or wrong" as from that special form of patriotism fostered among the English with the successive defections of Henry VIII and Elizabeth I from the Church of Rome. Rather, it consists in a love of his native country combined with the lamentation expressed by Gaunt in the three verbs that follow on the long subject, over the way the country has been misgoverned by its rulers, whether Richard II or the Tudors. Moreover, this deep-seated loyalty of the dramatist, to both England and Rome, that is, both his native country and its age-old religious tradition, is illustrated in certain annotations to an old copy of Edward Halle's *Chronicles*, which provided Shakespeare with one of the major sources for his history plays. The discovery of these annotations was made public in 1954 by a bookseller named Alan Keen, in a book he published with Roger Lubbock under the title *The Annotator*. When the copy came into Keen's possession, he was naturally interested in tracing its ownership, and his search brought him as far as the country mansion of Sir Thomas Hesketh at Rufford Hall. Hesketh had been named in the above-mentioned will of Alexander Houghton as a possible patron to the young William Shakeshafte. So mightn't the annotator, Keen wondered, be none other than the young William Shakespeare, while working on his plays of English history? In the annotations, moreover, Keen noticed two prominent qualities: the first, a love of the annotator's country as opposed to France, and the second, a love of the old Catholic faith as opposed to the new ideas of the reformers—in spite of the Protestant bias of the chronicler. The only problem was that the annotations were rather on the pages dealing with the reign of Henry V than on the subsequent reign of Henry VI, which covered the first three of Shakespeare's histories.

To explain this fact, it has to be remembered that when he was occupied with the composition of the three parts of *Henry VI*, Shakespeare was not yet the great master of dramaturgy he later became. He was still an apprentice in the art of drama, and in those days, even experienced dramatists, let alone apprentices, had to content themselves with "hack" writing in collaboration with others. Particularly when we consider these three parts of *Henry VI*, we find in them so much disorder, even chaos—as it were, reflecting the chaotic condition of that reign—that it is difficult to recognize in them the work of one author. Rather, the hands of several authors have been discerned in them, including the so-called university wits, Robert Greene and Thomas Nashe, who had been fellow students at St. John's College, Cambridge. No wonder Greene went on to warn his fellow Cambridge graduate Christopher Marlowe against the "upstart crow" he saw in the young Shakespeare. Incidentally, the date of Greene's *Groatsworth of Wit* (1592) happens to coincide with two contemporary references to the first part of *Henry VI*, one by Nashe himself in his *Piers Penniless* (referring to the victories of Sir John Talbot as English general in France), and the other by the theatre manager Philip Henslowe in his record of the play as performed by Strange's Men in that year.

There are, however, scholars who insist on the integrity of all the plays recognized as Shakespeare's by his fellow actors

John Heminge and Henry Condell, as co-editors of the First Folio of 1623. In their "Preface to the Reader" they emphasize that the plays "now offered to your view" are "cured and perfect of their limbs," in contrast to the previous quarto versions, and are "absolute in their numbers" as the author conceived them. Yet there remain serious misgivings about Shakespeare's part not only in the three plays of *Henry VI*, but also in *Titus Andronicus*, among his early plays. As for his later plays, the editors accepted *Henry VIII*, in which Shakespeare almost certainly collaborated with the young John Fletcher, but rejected *Two Noble Kinsmen*, which was also a collaborative effort with Fletcher, as well as *Pericles*, which came to be accepted as Shakespearian only in a reissue of the Third Folio in 1664. Thus it seems as if each play has to be considered on its own merits, without placing overmuch trust in the first actor-editors. Given the circumstances of the Elizabethan theatre, especially during Shakespeare's "apprentice" years, it is only natural that he should have been required to collaborate with others—even without their consent.

The best evidence, however, for multiple authorship in the first four plays of English history (covering the reigns of Henry VI, Edward IV, and Richard III) is to be found in the plays themselves. The three plays of *Henry VI*, for example, are so confusing and chaotic that while they no doubt reflect the chaos in the English history of that time, much of their chaos may be attributed to differences of style and viewpoint among the collaborators. As for Shakespeare's part in them, it is rather to be found here and there in the poetic imagery and versification of individual speeches than in the structure of the plays, which is perhaps what Greene meant by "borrowed feathers." It may also be found in the contrasting characters of the pious King Henry, on the one hand, and the ruthless Richard of Gloucester (the future Richard III), on the other. This is a contrast that stands out most vividly in the third part. On the one hand, we have the set speech of Henry as he retires from the field of battle at Towton, with a characteristic longing for rural peace (no doubt echoing the mind of the dramatist), "O God, methinks it were a happy life, / To be no better than a homely swain!" (ii.5). Then, on the other hand, we hear the Machiavellian ambitions of Richard, "I'll make my heaven to dream upon the crown, / And while I live, to account this world but hell"—culminating in his declaration, "I can add colours to the chameleon, / Change shapes with Proteus for advantages, / And set the murderous Machiavel to school" (iii.2). The same Richard goes on in the final act to murder Henry and to reject his Christian ideal of love: "And this word 'love', which greybeards call divine, / Be resident in men like one another / And not in me. I am myself alone" (v.6).

Richard III

The appeal of King Henry to the ideal of rustic life is interestingly echoed by the exiled duke in *As You Like It*, in his introduction to the Forest of Arden: "Now, my co-mates and brothers in exile, / Hath not old custom made this life more sweet / Than that of painted pomp?" (ii.1). It is in the same play that Shakespeare recalls the memory of Christopher Marlowe, who had been killed in a tavern by a fellow spy in 1593: "Dead shepherd, now I find thy saw of might. / Who ever lov'd that lov'd not at first sight?" (iii.5). It may well have been Marlowe's influence on him that made all the difference between the chaos of *Henry VI* in its three parts and the symmetrical order of *Richard III*. It is as if, through his contrasting characterization of Henry and Richard, Shakespeare is leading up to his first dramatic masterpiece in the later play. For in the regal ambition of Richard, from his opening soliloquy in *Richard III*, "Now is the winter of our discontent / Made glorious summer by this sun of York," and his barefaced determination "to prove a villain" (i.1), there is something characteristically Marlovian. From then onward everything in the play centers on Richard's ambition, as he surmounts obstacle upon obstacle, ridding himself first of his brother Clarence, then his other brother King Edward, then the little sons of Edward—till he is in turn defeated and killed at the battle of Bosworth by his rival Henry Tudor, Earl of Richmond. And so the Tudor dynasty replaces that of Plantagenet.

To this extent Shakespeare was no doubt indebted to Marlowe with his "mighty line"—indebted to the blown ambition of a Tamburlaine and the Machiavellian villainy of a Barabas (in *The Jew of Malta*). Yet he wasn't above satirizing his predecessor in the character of Pistol in the second part of *Henry IV*, with his swaggering reference to "hollow pamper'd jades of Asia" (echoing *Tamburlaine*). Nor is it unlikely that Marlowe, with his poem *Hero and Leander*, as continued by George Chapman in 1598, was the "rival poet" in Shakespeare's sonnets, with their mention of "the proud full sail of his great verse" (lxxxvi). Incidentally, it is noteworthy that to Marlowe in particular Greene had addressed his above-mentioned *Groatsworth of Wit*, warning him against this "Shakescene." Marlowe and Greene were Cambridge wits, not without links to the shady underworld of Cecilian espionage, in contrast to the noble circle within which Shakespeare moved, connected with two Catholic earls, Derby and Southampton, who were among the prime objects of that espionage.

Yet another, more tangible reason for the contrast between the chaos of the three parts of *Henry VI*—with their depiction of the contention between the houses of Lancaster and York—and the order of *Richard III* may be seen in relation to their respective sources. The chronicles on which Shakespeare relied were those of Holinshed and Halle, but for the play of *Richard III* he had the additional advantage of Sir Thomas More's *Life of King Richard III*, which had been written by 1513 but was not published till 1543. One thing that stands out in the play, more than the Machiavellianism of the villain, is the abundance of its religious and biblical references. Even the villain has his share in this abundance, so as to turn him into a religious hypocrite, as he himself confesses (in one of his soliloquies), "I seem a saint when most I play the devil" (i.3).

Already in the second scene, in the funeral procession for King Henry VI (whom he himself has murdered), there takes place a remarkable conversation between Richard and Lady Anne, who is chief mourner for her late father-in-law. It is as it were a continuation, from the foregoing contrast in Part III of *Henry VI*, between the same villain and the pious king. Whereas Anne's words are charged with reference to hell and devils, pointed at Richard, he merely responds by calling her, "Sweet saint, for charity," appealing to "the rules of charity, / Which renders good for bad, blessings for curses." He flatters her as "divine perfection of a woman," so as eventually to win her over, even to the extent of making her his wife. Yet once she has departed, he gloats over her, preening himself that, whereas she had "God, her conscience, and these bars against me, / And nothing I to back my suit withal / But the plain devil and dissembling looks," he has won her, "all the world to nothing!" (i.2). The same kind of suit he presses later in the play with the former queen of Edward IV, Elizabeth, even at a moment when she is most indignant with him, and yet he asks her to further his desire for marriage with her daughter—and she eventually consents. Then, once he has won her over, he exclaims after her, "Relenting fool, and shallow, changing woman!" (iv.4).

In connection with these two scenes, showing Richard's rhetorical skill in dealing with women, there are other parallel scenes of choric lament uttered against Richard by royal women. In the first, the part of Chorus is restricted to one woman, the widow of Henry VI, Queen Margaret, who hurls a series of curses at Richard, calling him "devil," "murderous villain," "cacodemon," "troubler of the poor world's peace," and "the slave of nature and the son of hell." She also directs her curses against the "poor painted queen" Elizabeth, Lord Hastings, the Duke of Buckingham, and other supporters of Richard (i.3). This scene is symmetrically balanced by a later one in which Margaret reappears with Queen Elizabeth and the Duchess of York, Richard's mother, who have all come, when it is too late, to realize the depths of his villainy. They now multiply their laments, as in the words of the duchess addressed no less to the old queen than to herself: "Dead life, blind sight, poor mortal living ghost, / Woe's scene, world's shame, grave's due by life usurp'd, / Brief abstract and record of tedious days!" (iv.4). Margaret further calls Richard "hell's black intelligencer" and continues, "Earth gapes, hell burns, fiends roar, saints pray, / To have him suddenly convey'd from hence." Yet it is then that Richard himself enters and wins over the widowed Queen Elizabeth as mentioned above.

Returning to the fourth scene, showing the death of Richard's brother Clarence at the hands of two murderers sent by him, it begins with a vivid description of the victim's dream of death by drowning—conjuring up the horrors of the recent Wars of the Roses, in which he has played a grisly part. On awakening he confesses, like the disciples of Christ in Gethsemani, "My soul is heavy, and I fain would sleep!" (cf. Matt xxvi.43). Then the murderers enter, though strangely religious—as it were, echoing Richard himself—in their approach to murder. Clarence himself appeals to their religious conscience, "I charge you, as you hope to have redemption / By Christ's dear blood shed for our grievous sins, / That you depart and lay no hands on me." When the second murderer tells him, "Make peace with God, for you must die, my lord," Clarence replies, "Hast thou that holy feeling in thy soul, / To counsel me to make my peace with God, / And art thou yet to thy own soul so blind?" But for all the victim's pleading, the deed is done, and immediately the murderer repents of his "bloody deed," adding—in a theme that runs through the plays from *Richard III* to *Macbeth*—"How fain, like Pilate, would I wash my hands / Of this most grievous murder!" (i.4).

The same religious spirit inspires the words of the dying King Edward, as he seeks to bring about a reconciliation of enemies among his courtiers. He tells them, "I every day expect an embassage / From my Redeemer to redeem me hence," but it is precisely then that Richard enters with the news of Clarence's death, which the king blames on himself and which now hastens his own death. On leaving, King Edward again makes mention of "the precious image of our dear Redeemer" (ii.1). From then onward violent deaths follow close on one another "in this our tottering state," "in this reeling world" (iii.2)—the deaths of Hastings, Buckingham, and the two little princes, sons of Edward—as it were, in fulfillment of Margaret's curses. Only when her curses are at last fulfilled is Richard himself exposed to the fate he has brought on so many victims in his ambition for the crown. The climax comes on the field of Bosworth, not so much in the battle itself as on the eve of battle—as we also see in the later play of *Henry V*—in the form of the successive ghosts of Richard's victims, who now come to pronounce curses on him but blessings on his opponent, Henry Tudor.

Interestingly, it is out of this situation that Richard, who has up till this moment been characterized, or rather caricatured, as a Machiavellian villain, at last becomes human, as the series of ghostly visitors succeed in touching his human conscience. For that is Shakespeare's genius, to look beyond the countenance to the conscience of his characters. Richard even wakens with a prayer, "Have mercy, Jesu!"—only to reflect, "Soft, I did but dream. / O coward conscience, how dost thou afflict me!" He even engages himself in an interior debate: "What! Do I fear myself? There's none else by. / Richard loves Richard. That is, I am I. / Is there a murderer here? No. Yes, I am." Then: "I am a villain. Yet I lie. I am not. / Fool, of thyself speak well. Fool, do not flatter." But in the end he can't help admitting, "My conscience hath a thousand several tongues, / And every tongue brings in a several tale, / And every tale condemns me for a villain." He even feels that, "there is no creature loves me, / And if I die, no soul will pity me." Richard may go on to take back what he has said, "Conscience is but a word that cowards use," and to urge his followers, "March on, join bravely, let us to't pell-mell, / If not to heaven, then hand in hand to hell." But at least for a brief moment the dark clouds have parted over him, to reveal in a melodramatic villain the heart of a human being.

Thus we may see in how many respects this early dramatic masterpiece of *Richard III* anticipates the later tragedies of *Hamlet* and *Macbeth*, not least in its use of such religious terms as "conscience" and "sin." Yet the villain's self-description before the beginning of the play remains true, "I am myself alone" (*Henry VI*, Part III, v.6). After all the chaos of the preceding plays on the Wars of the Roses, both the play and the character of Richard III stand out as at once Shakespearian and unique.

chapter 3
Apprentice in Comedy

▨ *The Comedy of Errors*

FOR AN APPRENTICE, Shakespeare came into his own with remarkable rapidity. From all the disorderly signs of collaboration in the three parts of *Henry VI*, adorned as they are with borrowed feathers, he emerges in *Richard III* with easy evidence of mastery—if with some indebtedness to Christopher Marlowe. Then in the same year as Strange's Men performed a play of "Henry VI" (1592), they also seem to have given a performance of *Titus Andronicus*. Here again we have signs of collaboration, both in the gruesome nature of this revenge play and in the evidence offered by a Restoration dramatist, Edward Ravenscroft, reporting the tradition that *Titus Andronicus* wasn't originally by Shakespeare but "brought in by a private author to be acted, and he only gave some master-touches to one or two of the principal parts or characters." Certainly, there are parts that seem to come from the pen of Shakespeare, but the conception of the whole is so gruesome that it reads like a parody of a genre that had already gone out of fashion and was already stale on the stage. That, apart from the history plays, is all Shakespeare has to contribute to the genre of tragedy till he comes, by way of romantic comedy, to the romantic tragedy of *Romeo and Juliet*.

Here the question suggests itself: Why in spite of his tragic Catholic background does the dramatic genius of Shakespeare turn at this time to the genre of comedy? For the history plays he had an abundant source of material in the two chronicles of Halle and Holinshed, and on that material (it may be imagined) he could always fall back in time of need. Elizabethan audiences, too, always seemed to be avid for such plays. Still, it looks as if Shakespeare's own dramatic preference in these early years of his career on the stage lay in the direction of comedy, if only by way of relief from the real tragedy surrounding him in Elizabethan life. So we have such plays as *The Comedy of Errors*, *The Two Gentlemen of Verona*, *The Taming of the Shrew*, and *Love's Labour's Lost*—in each of which scholars have detected some traces of collaboration, though the master-hand is apparent in them all. What is more, though these plays belong to the genre of comedy, few of them are without indications of tragedy— indications that, as Hippolyta says in *A Midsummer Night's Dream*, "grow to something of great constancy" (v.1).

This tragic background is most evident in what is commonly regarded as the first (and shortest) of Shakespeare's comedies, *The Comedy of Errors*. It is based on a play by the Roman comedian Plautus, *Menaechmi,* which may have been familiar to Shakespeare either from his schooldays at Stratford or from his schoolmastering in Lancashire, but he adapts the original Latin with considerable alterations of his own. Instead of the unfamiliar Epidamnum in Illyria, which is the setting for Plautus, he chooses Ephesus as being more familiar to his Christian audiences (from Acts xix and St. Paul's letter to the Ephesians). Then to the "errors" occasioned by two pairs of twins, masters and servants, who have been separated from birth but now coincidentally find themselves in the same city unknown to each other, he adds a sentence of death hanging over the head of an old merchant (father to one pair of twins) merely because he has come from Syracuse by shipwreck to the coast of Ephesus. The play begins with the imposition of his death sentence, in which he is allowed just one day to find a ransom. At the end of the day, because he has been unable to find the money, he is being led out to death.

In this way, it may be observed, Shakespeare begins his dramatic career with a play that maintains the classical unities of place, time, and action, and he ends it with another such play in *The Tempest*. Yet in between, in almost all the remaining plays, he swerves from those unities. In *The Comedy of Errors*, too, as in so many others, there is a tragic background of shipwreck, involving death and/or exile, which implicitly points to the other form of persecution for Elizabethan Catholics.

This addition by Shakespeare to the play of Plautus, of such enmity between Syracuse and Ephesus as incurs the death penalty for citizens of one city when caught in the other, is quite anachronistic in terms of historical setting. It takes on a degree of plausibility only when Syracuse is understood as Rome and Ephesus as London. In the time of Shakespeare it was indeed a crime punishable by death for a Catholic priest to be apprehended not only in London but anywhere in England. What is more, such a priest could come only in disguise, and a typical form of disguise, whether in attire or in correspondence, was that of a merchant. The particular background, too, chosen for the place of execution in Act V is "the melancholy vale, / The place of death and sorry execution, / Behind the ditches of the abbey here" (v.1), which has been identified as Shoreditch, near the old abbey of Holywell, the location not only of Shakespeare's old Theatre but also of the gallows for a seminary priest, William

Hartley, who was put to death here soon after the Armada was defeated in 1588. In the comedy, however, all ends happily through the intercession of the abbess Aemilia, who turns out to be the long-lost wife of the old merchant Aegeon. They are, moreover, the parents of the twin brothers Antipholus of Syracuse and Ephesus. So the confusions of the play are finally resolved.

Within the twofold plot of the play, in contrast to the plight of his merchant father, everything turns out miraculously in favor of the visiting Antipholus of Syracuse and his servant Dromio. Antipholus receives a warm welcome in the home of Adriana, wife to his twin brother of Ephesus, though there he is treated by her to a sermon on the proper relations of husband and wife (ii.2)—echoing the words of St. Paul in his letter to the Ephesians (v.22–33). There, too, he becomes enamoured of Adriana's sister, Luciana, whom he addresses as if she were the Virgin Mary herself: "Less in your knowledge and your grace you show not / Than our earth's wonder, more than earth, divine" (iii.2). For himself, however, and for his servant Dromio, "This is the fairyland," in which everything seems to happen at cross purposes, and they seem to be surrounded "with goblins, owls and elvish sprites" (ii.2). And so they feel like running away.

For the twin brother of Ephesus, however, everything turns out in his disfavor, till a climax is reached when he is treated as a madman and subjected to an exorcism by a conjuror named Pinch. The latter solemnly adjures him: "I charge thee, Satan, hous'd within this man, / To yield possession to my holy prayers, / And to thy state of darkness hie thee straight. / I conjure thee by all the saints in heaven" (iv.4). The whole episode seems to be a satire on certain Catholic exorcisms carried out in the neighborhood of London by the Jesuit William Weston and the seminary priest

Robert Dibdale (Shakespeare's former schoolmate from Shottery) in the mid-1580s. Yet the anti-Catholic satire is countered by the name of the exorcist, which echoes that of a contemporary Protestant critic of the exorcisms, Robert Phinch, author of *The Knowledge and Appearance of the Church* (1590). So we seem to have a case here of what Hamlet calls "the enginer / Hoist with his own petar" (iii.4).

The Taming of the Shrew

Another early comedy that has invariably met with success on the stage is *The Taming of the Shrew*. Presented as a play-within-the-play, it begins with an Induction showing a beggar being treated as a lord and offered this play for his entertainment. But we are never shown the outcome, as if in the end the dramatist has forgotten about the beginning. Here we seem to have no such tragic background as in *The Comedy of Errors*—until in Act IV we come to the mock warning given by Tranio to a pedant who has come from Mantua to Padua: "Of Mantua, sir! Marry, God forbid! / . . . 'Tis death for anyone in Mantua / To come to Padua"—which is the very situation of Syracusan merchants coming to Ephesus in the previous play. Otherwise, everything in the play is not just comic but farcical, in both plots—the one that shows the wooing of the fair Bianca by several suitors, notably the hero Lucentio with his clever servant Tranio, and the other the wooing of her shrewish sister Katharina by the masterful Petruchio.

The source of this play is disputed, owing to a problematic connection with the similarly titled *Taming of a Shrew*. There is, however, an interesting possibility of a connection, if more general, with one of Erasmus' *Colloquies* (translated into English, 1557): "A Merry Dialogue, declaring the properties of shrewd wives and honest wives," which in turn is said to have been inspired by Sir Thomas More's dealings with his shrewish wife, Alice. At least, on Petruchio's success in his taming of Katharina, his friend Hortensio echoes the very words of More, if spoken in a different context: "The field is won!" (iv.5). As for the other plot, in his wooing of Bianca, Lucentio comes to her on the pretext of tutoring her in the humanities, after he has been introduced to her father as "this young scholar, that hath been long studying at Rheims" (ii.1)—the very place where the seminarians of Douai had migrated for safety's sake in 1578.

So much of the humor in this play is derived from the use of disguise. Already in the Induction the beggar is disguised from himself in the clothing of a lord. Then the several suitors for the hand of Bianca have to resort to disguise in order to visit her and woo her, under her father's very nose. Lastly, the anonymous pedant is persuaded by the clever Tranio to pose as Lucentio's father, Vincentio, so as to assure Bianca's father of a rich dowry for his daughter—until the real Vincentio turns up! This motif of disguise we may carry even further, in view of the seemingly chance mention of Rheims, to the original motive of Lucentio in venturing from his home in Pisa to the university city of Padua. There, he explains, it is his intention to "institute / A course of learning and ingenious studies," but in fact he goes on to woo and win the fair Bianca. Such is also, as we will see, the situation of the "two gentlemen of Verona," who make their way to Milan only to fall in love with the fair Silvia. Such, too, is that of Bassanio in *The Merchant of Venice*, when he goes (with financial assistance from his friend Antonio) to Belmont to woo Lady Portia. Such, again, we may add, were the studies of the seminarians at Douai or Rheims or Rome, whither they had gone at no little risk to themselves and their families in search of a religious ideal, for love (it may be said) of the Virgin Mary.

The Two Gentlemen of Verona

There is a similar search at the beginning of the next comedy, *The Two Gentlemen of Verona*, when the hero Valentine tells his friend Proteus of his intention "[t]o see the wonders of the world abroad / Than living dully sluggardiz'd at home" (i.1). Such is also the mind of Proteus's father, Antonio, on due consultation with his cloistered brother, that his son "cannot be a perfect man, / Not being tried and tutor'd in the world" (i.3). Thus it is that both gentlemen, Valentine and Proteus, make their way to the duke's court at Milan, where they both fall in love with the duke's daughter Silvia—though Proteus already has a lover named Julia back in Verona. Julia in turn undertakes what she calls a "pilgrimage," in male disguise, to Milan, only to overhear Proteus's song in praise of Silvia: "Who is Silvia? What is she, / That all our swains commend her? / Holy, fair and wise is she, / The heaven such grace did lend her, / That she might admired be" (iv.2). As with Luciana, so with Silvia, there is an aura of mystery and grace, making her the object of a romantic quest for both gentlemen. To escape the duke's anger on learning of his love, Valentine takes refuge in the woods outside Milan, shortly to be followed by Silvia, also in male disguise, with the assistance of the romantic Sir Eglamour and the more practical Friar Patrick, "Out at the postern by the abbey-wall" (v.1)—despite the danger of being "attended by some spies." Thus the play may be seen as looking forward in various ways to *Romeo and Juliet* (though Juliet doesn't escape with Romeo), *A Midsummer Night's Dream* (though Hermia doesn't assume male disguise), and *As You Like It*, with its "shadowy desart, unfrequented woods" and "mansion" (like Wroxhall Abbey) "growing ruinous" and "leaving no memory of what it was" (v.4).

At the end of the play, however, Valentine's declaration to his friend, within the hearing of both heroines in disguise, "All that was mine in Silvia I give thee" (v.4), is no less shocking to poor Julia, who swoons at his words, than to modern feminists. It is also of a piece with the ending to *The Taming of the Shrew*, in which the subdued Katharina gives a lesson in wifely obedience to the other wives, who fail to come at the command of their respective husbands (v.2). It is hardly enough to say that Shakespeare is merely conforming himself to the male chauvinistic ideas of his age, since, from a human viewpoint, he must have been aware of the awkwardness of such endings. The only satisfactory explanation—apart from Dr. Johnson's idea that the dramatist was hastening to finish the play—is that he is looking from a natural to a supernatural level of meaning, according to Chesterton's observation about his plays in general, "Man was natural, but woman was supernatural."

■ *Love's Labour's Lost*

The last of the "apprentice" comedies is *Love's Labour's Lost*, which is one of the few plays by Shakespeare (with *A Midsummer Night's Dream* and *The Tempest*) without any identifiable source. It is a highly esoteric play, evidently written not for the public theatre but for a small coterie of friends, including the two Catholic earls of Southampton (as patrons of Shakespeare's poems) and Derby (as patron of his plays). The plot centers on the project of an academy undertaken by Ferdinand, king of Navarre—echoing the personal name of Ferdinando, Lord Strange, soon to become Earl of Derby and king of Man on his father's death in 1593. In France at that time there happened to be two such royal academies, one in Paris under the auspices of the Catholic Henry III, king of France, and the other in Nerac under the auspices of the Protestant Henry of Bourbon, king of Navarre. The names of the lords who figure at Shakespeare's academy are all chosen from the leaders in the religious strife of the time, with Biron and Longueville on the Protestant side and Mayenne on the Catholic side—to give them their French spellings. There was also an academy in London, under the auspices of Lord Burghley, as Master of the Wards, for such noble wards of his as the earls of Essex, Rutland, and Southampton, with the double aim of indoctrinating them in Protestantism and lining his own pocket—though in the outcome he incurred only their strong dislike. According to the royal plan, the lords are expected to take vows not of monastic but of academic seclusion from the world, especially from the company of women, but they immediately go on to break their vows with the arrival at the king's court of the Princess of France with her three ladies.

Implicit in the play, scholars have discerned many topical meanings, on which I have barely touched. First, in connection with the original purpose of academic study, we have the ideal of grace incarnated in the Princess of France, as being the principal heroine, who is addressed by her courtier Boyet, "Be now as prodigal of all dear grace / As Nature was in making graces dear" (ii.1). Then, in the sad outcome, after the announcement of the death of the king, her father—an unexpected outcome for a comedy—she translates that ideal into practical charity, which she and her ladies proceed to require of their noble hosts, if they are to make "a world-without-end bargain" with them in marriage (v.2). Before all this comes about, however, and after the vows of the lords have been successively broken and exposed, one of the lords, Berowne (for Biron), eloquently praises the ideal of love in a Platonic rather than a Christian sense, including an implied reference to Shakespeare as poet of the sonnets:

"Never durst poet touch a pen to write / Until his ink were temper'd with love's sighs" (iv.3). It is the Platonic ideal of the academy, as maintained in the contemporary work of Pierre de la Primaudaye, *The French Academy* (English translation, 1586), which is subsequently tempered by the more practical Christian insistence on works of charity—such as were even then being realized in the Catholic religious congregations founded in Rome for the care of the sick, notably that of St. Camillus de Lellis authorized by Pope Gregory XIV in 1591.

Also previous to the end we may notice the strange presentation of the "Nine Worthies" by the minor characters in the play—as it were, anticipating that of "Pyramus and Thisbe" by the Athenian workmen at the end of *A Midsummer Night's Dream*. The actors are here rudely abused by the noble lords, most of all the pedant Holofernes, who takes the part of Judas Maccabaeus but is willfully mistaken by them as Judas Iscariot. This looks like an esoteric reference to John Florio, the Italian tutor and secretary to the young Earl of Southampton but reputedly imposed as a spy on the earl's household by Lord Burghley—as in the later play Macbeth tells his wife, "There's not a one of them but in his house / I keep a servant fee'd" (*Macbeth* iii.4). Thus the baiting of Holofernes as Judas would have had a specially acceptable implication to Shakespeare's patron, against which Florio himself could hardly object without acknowledging the identification.

chapter 4
Annus Mirabilis

Romeo and Juliet

I𝗍 IS DIFFICULT to determine the precise dating of any of
Shakespeare's plays. There is such a difference between the
first inspiration, the actual composition, and the first performance. As T. S. Eliot observes in "The Hollow Men,"
"Between the conception and the creation / Between the
emotion and the response / Falls the shadow." That is the
shadow of ignorance. Ben Jonson is responsible for the criticism that Shakespeare in his writing "never blotted out a
line" and that he had such "an excellent fancy, brave notions,
and gentle expressions" and "flowed with that facility, that
sometimes it was necessary he should be stopped" (*Discoveries*). This needn't mean, however, that the dramatist never
put his pen aside till the play he happened to be engaged in
was completed, or that there mightn't be years between the
beginning and the end of one play—as we may well conjec-
ture in the case of *Macbeth*—or that he mightn't have left a
play unfinished—as seems to have been the case with *Timon
of Athens.* Yet there is one year, 1595, for which most scholars
agree on the dating of three notably lyrical plays, the tragedy
of *Romeo and Juliet,* the comedy of *A Midsummer Night's
Dream,* and the history play of *Richard II.* It is a year that

may aptly be called Shakespeare's *annus mirabilis*—his year of wonders.

To begin with the most famous and most lyrical play, *Romeo and Juliet*, its lyrical quality is evident from the opening Chorus, or Prologue, which takes the unusual form of a sonnet. The same is true of the Chorus, or Prologue, to Act II, though a chorus is appended to none of the subsequent acts. It seems as if the poet-dramatist is still riding the wave of inspiration for the series of sonnets that are commonly regarded as dedicated to his noble patron, the young Earl of Southampton, and accordingly dated 1593–94, following the dates of the two long poems, *Venus and Adonis* and *The Rape of Lucrece*, which are both dedicated to that young man. The same sonnet form is interestingly repeated by Romeo and Juliet in their opening dialogue or duet on their meeting in the house of her father Capulet, appearing in the rhyme scheme from Romeo's "If I profane with my unworthiest hand" down to "while my prayer's effect I take" (i.5).

The tragic situation from which the events of the play take their rise, the enmity between the households of Capulet and Montague in "fair Verona," strangely echoes the similar setting for other early plays of Shakespeare. It is what we have already seen in England during the Wars of the Roses as featured in the three parts of *Henry VI*, in Rome under Saturninus and Bassianus as portrayed in *Titus Andronicus*, in Ephesus as opposed to Syracuse in *The Comedy of Errors*, and in the supposed relation (as asserted by Tranio) between Mantua and Padua in *The Taming of the Shrew*. Needless to say, for Shakespeare the archetype for all these oppositions is that between Catholic and Protestant, even within one and the same family, in his native England.

From the outset the lovelorn Romeo is persuaded to go to Capulet's ball only in the hope of meeting his lady-love

Rosaline there. There, however, he meets not Rosaline, who is too far above him in his fond imagination, but Juliet, of whom he subsequently tells Friar Laurence, "She, whom I love now, / Doth grace for grace and love for love allow" (ii.3). In other words, as with so many of Shakespeare's lovers, Romeo sees in Juliet an incarnation of divine grace, prompting him even to echo the words of St. John on the incarnate Word of God: "Of his fullness have all we received, and grace for grace" (Jn 1:16). Even his way to her presence he regards in terms of a pilgrimage, as in the above-mentioned conversation with her: "If I profane with my unworthiest hand / This holy shrine . . . / My lips, two blushing pilgrims," while Juliet for her part encourages him with the same imagery: "Good pilgrim . . . / For saints have hands that pilgrims' hands do touch, / And palm to palm is holy palmers' kiss" (i.5). Thus Juliet is to Romeo as Silvia is to Valentine and Proteus, as Portia is to Bassanio and the Prince of Morocco—the object of a holy pilgrimage and a type of the Virgin Mary. And in the same way Juliet may be seen as corresponding to the ideal of English students from Warwickshire and Lancashire making their perilous way to the seminary beyond the seas.

The very house to which Romeo belongs, and to which Juliet objects with the words "O be some other name!" is indeed that which the dramatist found in his source, Arthur Brooke's poetic version, *Romeus and Juliet* (1562); but for Shakespeare the house must have had a further association with the name of the Catholic nobleman Viscount Montague, grandfather to the young Earl of Southampton. As for Juliet's house of Capulet, whose name features in the same source, it is also mentioned in the play under the alternative form of "Capel," as "Capel's monument" (v.1)—a not uncommon surname and even place-name in Hampshire and West Sussex. Of course, in Verona the strife is merely personal and political, as in many Italian cities of that time, while all are united in the one Catholic Church and in respect for Friar Laurence. Unlike the various parsons who appear in the plays, such as Sir Nathaniel in *Love's Labour's Lost*, this friar has the respect not only of the two lovers, for whom he is their spiritual father, but also of Capulet, who praises him as "this reverend holy friar" (iv.1), and of the Prince, who assures him, "We still have known thee for a holy man" (v.3). On the other hand, in the Protestant source, Brooke constantly blames him as pander to the lovers and chief cause of their misfortune.

Further, the ideal of romantic love, as presented in this pair of lovers, is upheld by Friar Laurence, both as he foresees in their alliance a means "to turn your households' rancour to pure love" (ii.3) and as he goes on to represent "holy Church" by incorporating "two in one" (ii.6). On the other hand, the ideal is almost immediately broken by the "rude will" of Romeo, in contrast to the "grace" of Juliet (ii.3), when, as a result of Romeo's untimely intervention, his friend Mercutio is killed by Juliet's cousin Tybalt. Before he dies, Mercutio calls down "a plague o' both your houses!"— words that have been applied, not without reason, to the religious controversies of the age. From this point of view, it might seem as if the dramatist is equally opposed to Catholic and Protestant, when they fall to mutual bickering. It is a meaning that seems to be borne out by the other words put into Helena's mouth in the contemporary comedy of *A Midsummer Night's Dream*: "When truth kills truth, O devilish-holy fray!" (iii.2), and by those put into the mouth of Lucio in *Measure for Measure*: "Grace is grace, despite of all controversy!" (i.2). No doubt, Shakespeare was all in favor of religious peace, but who, it may be asked, first introduced the element of strife, when all was at peace in the Christian world before the religious changes were introduced by a king whose aim in introducing them was as much secular as religious?

A Midsummer Night's Dream

On this point of religious peace, we may proceed to the above-mentioned comedy of *A Midsummer Night's Dream*. Here we seem to be far from the real world of religious strife, among the fairies who inhabit the wood outside Athens, representing the ancient pagan religion under the kindly patronage of Oberon and Titania (or Diana). Yet even between Oberon and Titania, even from the outset of the play, we hear of strife, in terms of a marital quarrel, as a result of which the human world is also in a state of confusion. This is typical of the beginning of almost all Shakespeare's plays at this time. On the human level, it seems as if harmony is prevailing between Theseus and Hippolyta, who are now preparing for their wedding day, but this has come about only as a result of wars undertaken by him against her as queen of the Amazons, and on the fairy level Theseus and Hippolyta correspond to Oberon and Titania. Then, too, before Theseus and Hippolyta can proceed to their wedding, they are faced with the problem of Lysander and Hermia, and of Demetrius and Helena, as Demetrius, though formerly committed to Helena, now claims the hand of Hermia in marriage, and his claim is supported by her father, Egeus. Thus from the beginning, as in *The Comedy of Errors*, the threat of death hangs over the head of Hermia, if she persists in her refusal to obey her father and marry Demetrius, but she insists on her loyalty to Lysander. A means of escape is offered her by Theseus: "To live a barren sister all your life, / Chanting faint hymns to the cold fruitless moon" (i.1), but she prefers the other expedient suggested by Lysander, that of flight into the forest outside Athens—recalling the way chosen by Valentine and Silvia in *The Two Gentlemen of Verona.*

That might have been a perfect solution for the time being, except that Hermia, being a woman, must go and tell her friend Helena, who in turn goes and tells Demetrius. (As Rosalind says in *As You Like It,* "Do you not know I am a woman? When I think, I must speak" [iii.2].) So they all follow each other into the wood that night. There the fairies are also gathering, as well as a group of Athenian tradesmen who are practicing a play to be presented before the duke and duchess on their wedding night. This is when Puck, Oberon's mischievous assistant, sprinkles the juice of "Cupid's flower," or Love-in-Idleness, on the eyes of Lysander, Demetrius, and Titania, with the result that Lysander falls in love with Helena instead of Hermia, and Demetrius also falls in love with Helena, while Titania falls in love with the absurd Bottom the Weaver, one of the Athenian tradesmen, now wearing the ass-head Puck has put over him. In this way all the preceding confusion is worse confounded. And now it is that the seemingly chance word put into the mouth of Helena, as quoted above, imparts to the whole situation a strangely contemporary relevance. Thus we may come to think of Athens in terms of Stratford, and the wood in terms of the Forest of Arden—with the dramatist's amused comment on it all, in the words of Puck, "Lord, what fools these mortals be!" (iii.2).

On the other hand, all is restored by means of the other juice of "Dian's bud," the power of chastity over that of cupidity, and the lovers come to themselves, waking up, as it were, from a nightmare, when, as Demetrius exclaims, "These things seem small and undistinguishable, / Like far-off mountains turned into clouds" (iv.1). All seems like a dream, not only for the lovers but also for Bottom, who recalls his night spent in the arms of Titania in almost Pauline terms: "The eye of man hath not heard, the ear of man hath not seen, man's hand is not able to taste, his tongue to conceive, nor his heart to report, what my dream was." So St. Paul speaks of his heavenly vision to the Corinthians (II Cor xii.2–4). To Puritan ears his words must sound little short of blasphemous, and yet they point to a deep, "bottomless" meaning, as Bottom himself declares: "It shall be called Bottom's Dream, because it hath no bottom" (iv.1). The rationalist Theseus, subsequently commenting on what he has just heard from the lovers, says, "The lunatic, the lover and the poet, / Are of imagination all compact," which sounds like a comment on and a response to the challenge of the Jesuit poet Robert Southwell in his dedication of his poems (published that very year, 1595) "to my worthy good cousin, Master W. S." Southwell says, "A poet, a lover and a liar are by many reckoned but three words of one signification," and the response of Shakespeare may be found in the words of Hippolyta to Theseus, where she justifies "the story of the night" with all its "fancy's images," inasmuch as they all "grow to something of great constancy" (v.1).

The final scene, which so appealed to the imagination of that great Shakespearian critic G. K. Chesterton (see his essay "A Midsummer Night's Dream" in *The Common Man*, 1950), contains the inimitable play-within-the-play presented by Bottom and the Athenian tradesmen. (Here it is noteworthy how much better is the behavior of the aristocratic lovers than the French lords on a similar occasion in *Love's Labour's Lost*.) When all is over, the fairies return to bless the house and the marriage beds in a ceremony that strangely recalls the old mediaeval rite of *Benedictio Thalami* in the Sarum Use. The moral of the play is that drawn by Puck, as in the similarly titled play by the Spanish playwright Calderon, that human life is but a dream—anticipating the words of Prospero at the end of *The Tempest*: "We are such stuff / As dreams are made on, and our little life / Is rounded with a sleep" (iv.1). Both speakers, it may be added, look back not so much to the old pagan days of Britain as to bygone mediaeval times. As the Anglican bishop of Norwich, Richard Corbet, lamented in his poem "Farewell to the Fairies," in the early seventeenth century, the fairies have passed with the passing of the old abbeys, when "their songs were Ave-Maries, / Their dances were procession."

■ *Richard II*

This nostalgia reappears in yet another form in the history play, or "tragedy," of *Richard II*, in the above-mentioned speech of John of Gaunt on "this England." What is all too often overlooked concerning this speech by superficial critics like Graham Greene (who imagines the dramatist as a jingoist) is that the long succession of epithets in praise of England is followed by three verbs expressive of lament: "is now leas'd out . . . is now bound in . . . hath made a shameful conquest of itself" (ii.1). This lament is explicitly applied to Richard's England, but it is no less applicable from a Catholic viewpoint to the England of Queen Elizabeth. A similar feeling is expressed in the recurrent theme of exile or banishment—first with reference to the son of Gaunt, Henry Bolingbroke, who must, owing to the king's unjust command, "tread the stranger paths of banishment" (i.3), then with reference to Richard himself, when the tables are turned on him and he is deposed and imprisoned in Pomfret Castle. Then, as Richard goes not to banishment but to imprisonment, he meets his weeping queen Isabella and exhorts her,

"Hie thee to France, / And cloister thee in some religious house. / Our holy lives must win a new world's crown" (v.1). Here is a theme that strangely echoes the similar theme in the other two plays of Shakespeare's *annus mirabilis*, when Romeo laments his banishment from Verona and Juliet (*Romeo and Juliet* iii.3) and when Hermia and Lysander face a similar banishment from Athens (*A Midsummer Night's Dream* i.1)—the lot, it may be remembered, of so many Catholic exiles in the reign of Queen Elizabeth. In all these plays, moreover, we find the religious life recommended to the heroine, as when Friar Laurence also proposes to place Juliet "among a sisterhood of holy nuns" (v.3) and when Theseus offers Hermia the option of being "in shady cloister mew'd" in a paradoxically "maiden pilgrimage" (i.1).

Returning to *Richard II*, it is noteworthy how the king changes from a secular, wayward youth to an increasingly religious way of thinking in his downfall—as it were, anticipating the case of Wolsey in *Henry VIII*, when in his fall "he felt himself, / And found the blessedness of being little" (iv.2). Formerly the only doctrine that appealed to him was that "divine right of kings" on which Henry VIII laid such exaggerated emphasis to justify his breach with Rome. But now, both in the deposition scene in Westminster Hall and in his imprisonment in Pomfret Castle, Richard sees himself as a figure of Christ in his passion, surrounded by enemies like Judas and Pilate. Of them he declares, "Did they not sometime cry, 'All hail!' to me? / So Judas did to Christ" (iv.1) and again, "Though some of you with Pilate wash your hands, / Showing an outward pity, yet you Pilates / Have here deliver'd me to my sour cross, / And water cannot wash away your sin." Thus he looks at once back to Clarence in *Richard III* (i.4) and forward to *Macbeth* (ii.2), with reference not only to the Bible but also to the mediaeval Passion play.

In his imprisonment Richard is more than ever devoted to thoughts of religion, as when in his mind he intermingles "thoughts of things divine . . . with scruples," as in the contrasting words of Jesus, inviting him with "Come, little ones" (cf. Matt xi.28) and yet repelling him with "It is as hard to come as for a camel / To thread the postern of a needle's eye" (cf. Matt xix.24). But the latter forbidding word hardly applies to him in prison, reduced as he is from king to beggar, from the possession of all to the condition of nothing. That, he now realizes—as it were, in anticipation of King Lear—is what he is. For "whate'er I be, / Nor I nor any man that but man is / With nothing shall be pleas'd, till he be eas'd / With being nothing" (v.5). Such is the enlightenment that comes to Richard when he has lost everything, and when he at last comes to himself. This isn't mere nothing, however, as Lear also comes to realize. Rather, the "nothing" is immediately qualified by the recognition of "love," even if it is only the imperfect expression of love in the discordant music he hears outside his prison walls. That, he admits, is at least "a sign of love, and love to Richard / Is a strange brooch in this all-hating world" (v.5)—in striking contrast to that rejection of love by his namesake, Richard III (*Henry VI*, Part III, v.6). From this play Shakespeare goes on to develop this all-important theme in *Much Ado About Nothing* (as proclaimed in the very title), in *Hamlet* and *King Lear*, and above all in the unfinished play of *Timon of Athens*, whose misanthropic hero dies in the recognition that "nothing brings me all things" (v.1).

chapter 5
Falstaff

 *Henry IV*, Part I

LET ME BEGIN with a word of protest against the categorization of Shakespeare's plays—problem plays, Roman plays, great tragedies, and so on. This also includes the custom, popularized by E. M. W. Tillyard, of dividing the plays on English history into two tetralogies, from the reign of Richard II until that of Richard III—omitting the earlier play of *King John* and the final historical "romance" of *Henry VIII*. Not that I would deny the convenience of such groupings, of which I have myself taken advantage in the past, but their greater inconvenience consists in the way they blur the distinctive quality of each play and put together what had better be left asunder. For Shakespeare in all his authentic plays is nothing if not unique.

To take the so-called first tetralogy, comprising the three parts of *Henry VI* followed by *Richard III*, I wonder if it could have been conceived by the dramatist himself from the outset as a group of four. Even as an effort at collaboration, there is so much disunity and disorder in the first three parts that they hardly make a whole, except under the name of the ineffectual king who presided over the events recorded in his reign. Then after so much disorder, to come upon the symmetrical arrangement of episodes in the fourth play is like—like what? Well, like passing from the work of the university wits to that of William Shakespeare, or at least from the work of an apprentice who isn't yet relied upon to produce a work of his own to that of a recognized master. Then, depending on one's dating of *King John*, there seems to have been a relapse on Shakespeare's part from his dramatic achievement in *Richard III* to another bland piece of dramaturgy in a play whose only notable scene is that in which little Arthur pleads with Hubert to spare his eyes. Even so, the scene is sufficiently similar to the parallel scene in the source-play, *The Troublesome Reign of King John*, to make us question both the originality and the authenticity of Shakespeare's *King John*.

Then it is said that Shakespeare enters upon his second tetralogy with *Richard II*, which I have treated separately because that is what it deserves. Unlike the other plays of English history, and yet in a deeper sense like them, *Richard II* is a really unique play and fully deserves to be ranked with *Romeo and Juliet* and *A Midsummer Night's Dream* for its lyricism rather than with other history plays for the mere chronicle record. Another quality in which this play stands out as unique is its lack of any real subplot that might justify a relapse from verse into prose. From start to finish this play is all verse. If it is to be correlated with another history play, I would choose *Richard III*, if only because these are the two plays of English history that bear the title "tragedy" in their first printed editions. As for the two parts of *Henry IV*, which follow in merely chronological order, they are rather to be classified as comedies, owing to the prevailing presence in them of Shakespeare's great comic creation, Sir John Falstaff. For this reason these two parts are in turn specifically different from the next historical play of *Henry V*, which belongs (in my opinion) to yet another *annus mirabilis* for the dramatist.

Putting aside, then, the concepts of tetralogy and even trilogy, we may turn to the two parts of *Henry IV* with the emphasis they deserve on the character of Sir John Falstaff. If Chaucer's poetic genius in *The Canterbury Tales* stands out (among other reasons) for his comic characterization of the Wife of Bath, the same may be said of Shakespeare's dramatic genius in his characterization of Falstaff. Hitherto in his comedies we have noted the characters of Petruchio in *The Taming of the Shrew*, Puck and Bottom in *A Midsummer Night's Dream*, and even in the tragedy of *Romeo and Juliet* such comic characters as Romeo's friend Mercutio and Juliet's unnamed Nurse. The success of Falstaff on the stage may have been responsible for the first appearance of the author's name on the title page of his printed plays, namely the 1598 quarto of *Love's Labour's Lost*—as it were, implying that his name has at last acquired market value. Also, according to tradition, it was thanks to Falstaff that Shakespeare could count the queen herself among his admirers. Even Shakespeare scholars have lost their hearts, and their minds, to him, as when A. C. Bradley wept bitter tears over what he called, "the rejection of Falstaff" in his well-known lecture of the same name (1909). More recently, at the end of the same century, the American scholar Harold Bloom placed Falstaff by the side of Hamlet as Shakespeare's two great characters and as prime instances of what he calls "the invention of the human" (see *The Invention of the Human*, Bloom's best-selling book, 1998).

Then, we may ask, how did Shakespeare come to conceive such an outstanding character for the two parts of *Henry IV*? The story of Prince Hal as "the wayward prince" was already present in the chronicles that provided the dramatist with the

main source of his history plays, and it had already been
dramatized in an anonymous play, which may have been
Shakespeare's immediate source, *The Famous Victories of
Henry V.* Moreover, the dramatic tradition of morality plays,
which Shakespeare inherited from the late Middle Ages, may
well have suggested to his mind that if there is a wayward
prince, there must also be a Vice of Waywardness. Or rather,
if Prince Hal is a prodigal son, as in Christ's parable, there
must also be a Vice of Prodigality. Such indeed is the way Falstaff is himself mockingly described by Prince Hal as "that
reverend Vice, that grey Iniquity, that father Ruffian, that
Vanity in years" (Part I, ii.4). In particular, among the traditional Seven Deadly Sins, Falstaff would stand for those of
Gluttony and Drunkenness, which were notoriously the easi-
est to caricature whether on the stage or in the pulpit. What is
more, there is a historical origin for Falstaff in the Lollard
champion, Sir John Oldcastle, whose very name survives in
the first scene in which Falstaff appears, when the prince hails
him as "my old lad of the castle" (i.2). Not only was Oldcastle
a Lollard, or follower of John Wycliffe, but he was also hailed
by John Foxe in his *Book of Martyrs* (1563) as "morning-star"
of the English Reformation. Here, however, Shakespeare is
lampooning him and making him a laughingstock both
among Elizabethan spectators and before the queen herself,
which may be regarded as a sign that the dramatist takes his
stand on the Papist rather than the Puritan side of the Reformation controversies. This preference of the dramatist was
noted by the Jesuit Robert Persons in his critique of Foxe's
book in *Three Conversions of England* (1603–4), which led the
Protestant historian John Speed in his *History of Great Britain*
(1611) to link their names as "the papist and his poet."

The actual introduction of Falstaff on the stage in the
second scene of Part I is impressive. First, we have to wade

through the heavy political problems weighing on the mind of the weary King Henry, made even heavier for him by the loose behavior of his wayward son, the Prince of Wales. Then, by contrast, we are shown Falstaff first asleep on a bench, then waking up on the prince's approach. "Now, Hal," he asks in all innocence, "what time of day is it, lad?" Appropriately the prince replies, "What a devil hast thou to do with the time of the day?" Such problems as that of time are for political personages to worry about, but as a comic Vice, Falstaff is above the passing of time. About him there is something eternal, as he goes on to indicate with an unending stream of quotations from the Bible, in keeping with his historical origin as a Lollard. He even makes a prayer, as if for the prince with reference to his companion Poins, in a parody of the Elizabethan Book of Common Prayer, "God give thee a spirit of persuasion and him the ears of profiting, that what thou speakest may move, and what he hears may be believed." For all his association with Poins, however, he makes the teasing remark, implying a Lutheran affiliation: "O if men were to be saved by merit, what hole in hell were hot enough for him?" (i.2). That is to say, how fortunate it is for Poins if Luther's teaching is to be believed, that he may yet be saved by faith alone.

Further, it may be added that in Falstaff we have an essentially prosaic character, belonging as he does (like Bottom) to low life, and so the scenes in which he appears are all—unlike any in *Richard II*—in prose. Still, the dramatist skillfully intersperses the political scenes, centering on the king and his troubles, with the comic scenes, featuring Falstaff and his companions (including the prince), in a pleasing alternation of verse and prose. As for Prince Hal, the future King Henry V, his preferences are for the time being on the side of low life, though from the outset he affirms his understanding of the class distinction between himself as prince and his plebeian friends, in a speech of almost incredible snobbishness: "I know you all, and will awhile uphold / The unyok'd humour of your idleness" (i.2). At the same time, he is gradually being drawn away from such unworthy associations by a sense of rivalry with the chivalrous son of the Earl of Northumberland, Henry Hotspur. Here we have two contrasting pairs, as central to the twofold plot of the play. First, there is the prodigal son with the personified Vice of Prodigality, Prince Hal and Falstaff. Second, there are the two Henrys: the gallant Hotspur in the north, who breaks out into open rebellion against the king, and Prince Hal in the south, who has been living in dishonor but eventually comes out on his father's side and defeats his rival. All the time, however, we are aware of his professed aim—echoing St. Paul's words to the Ephesians (v.16)—of "redeeming the time."

In this way, the first part of *Henry IV* is not without a structure, as it might have been if all had been left in Falstaff's hands. Rather, it assumes a clear form with events in the outside world moving to a climax when the rebels come into armed conflict with the forces of the king. Yet even the battle fought at Shrewsbury is not without comic scenes, as Falstaff follows Prince Hal to the battlefield and even claims the honor of having achieved what the prince has already achieved, namely, victory in single combat over Henry Hotspur. All the time, however, our sympathies are gradually being withdrawn from the funny man, as we are shown something sinister behind his idle dallying with "wine, women and song." He may excuse himself as "poor Jack Falstaff," representing the old Adam no longer "in the state of innocency" but now "in the days of villainy" (iii.3). He may plead his "more frailty" owing to being weighed down with

"more flesh than another man." But once he finds himself in
a position of authority and in charge of "the king's press," for
the enforcing of military service, he is more than willing to
take bribes from those who can afford it. Those who remain
he despises as "a hundred and fifty tattered prodigals, lately
come from swine-keeping, from eating draff and husks,"
mere "food for powder," or what we call "cannon fodder"—
for which, as he himself ingenuously admits, "I have misused
the king's press damnably" (iv.2). When we finally get to the
field of battle, it all seems great fun when Falstaff proves himself a mere coward and yet pretends to the honor of having
killed Henry Hotspur, even to the face of Prince Hal, who
has just achieved that honor. This is the context in which he
makes his famous "catechism of honor," rejecting that ideal
whether as personified in Hotspur or in Prince Hal, concluding, "I'll none of it!" In him there may be humor without
honor, and he may prefer (with the Beatles) to "make love,
not war," but when humor (in both senses of the word)
makes a rascal of him, in the taking of bribes and letting his
men get "peppered" in battle, one can hardly praise or
indulge him—as critics like Bradley and Bloom are all too
ready to do—for being such a scoundrel.

▪ *Henry IV*, Part II

On passing from Part I to Part II of *Henry IV*, we may feel
we have put behind us all that was most amiable in Falstaff,
not least his unashamed roguery. He himself seems to put in
a protest, in the dramatist's name, against having to reappear
in this sequel. As he complains in the second scene, "It was
always yet the trick of our English nation, if they have a
good thing" (meaning himself) "to make it too common,"
adding, "If you will needs say I am an old man, you should
give me rest" (i.2). Evidently, he was so popular in Part I

that the gratified spectators clamored, like Oliver, for more, and the dramatist found himself reduced to the necessity of providing them with a repeat performance, while somehow coming out with something new. So we may now see it as one of his principal aims not so much to please his audience with repetition as to prepare their minds for the eventual rejection of Falstaff by the newly crowned King Henry V. This he does partly by emphasizing the disreputable aspect of his comic character and partly by keeping him away from the prince's company. Here we see Falstaff recognizing the name of one of his diseases as "consumption of the purse" while looking for its cure in turning the disease "to commodity" with a good wit. His idleness is not to be bought without a price.

This decline in Falstaff's character in Part II (though it has already begun in Part I) is marked in several stages. From the time of his appearance in the second scene, he makes his boast—all too often quoted by his fans out of context—"The brain of this foolish-compounded clay, man, is not able to invent anything that tends to laughter, more than I invent or is invented on me. I am not only witty in myself, but the cause that wit is in other men" (i.2). So far from being witty, however, such a boast is merely a sign of the pride that comes before a fall. Nor is it long before the Lord Chief Justice enters and upbraids him for having "misled the youthful prince." Nor is the lord deceived by Falstaff's tongue, which is ever ready with words of self-justification. The lord merely comments, "Fie, fie, fie, Sir John!" and leaves it at that—with what we might think is commendable tolerance. In the next Falstaff scene, however, we find the rogue being sought by two officers of the law, sinisterly named Fang and Snare, at the suit of his hostess Dame Quickly, and the Chief Justice is again present. Yet again

Falstaff proves his skill in words by appeasing the hostess, though not the Chief Justice, who comments, "Thou art a great fool!" (ii.1). Prince Hal and his friend Poins later come in disguised as servants for Hal's first and last meeting with Falstaff in the play, which takes place that night. For this occasion the dramatist introduces two new characters: the braggart soldier Pistol, who delights in declaiming meaningless bits and pieces of Marlovian verse, and the prostitute Doll Tearsheet. This degenerates into an ugly scene with Falstaff and Pistol drawing swords on each other—as though recalling the incident when Marlowe himself was set upon by fellow spies and killed in a tavern at Deptford in 1593. In the outcome the prince is disgusted and tells Poins (in a brief reversion to blank verse), "I feel me much to blame, / So idly to profane the precious time" (ii.4).

In these words one may sense an echo of what the poet has already told his friend, if in a different sense, in the sonnet "Let me confess that we two must be twain" (xxxvi). From now on Prince Hal has to deal with more serious matters, which percolate down to him from the main plot of political events. Now again he has to face a rebellion from the north, this time from the archbishop of York, Richard Scroop. But this time the rebellion is put down without any battle, by a deceptive trick played on the rebels by Hal's brother Prince John of Lancaster. Yet again Falstaff takes advantage of the rebellion to misuse the "king's press," going to the countryside of Gloucestershire, not far from Shakespeare's hometown of Stratford. There he meets an old friend, Justice Shallow, with whom he indulges in memories of youthful escapades—which seem to bring them both back to life. In Shallow, it is commonly said, the dramatist is satirizing his old Protestant enemy, Sir Thomas Lucy, who had been entrusted by the Earl of Leicester with the task of prosecuting the Arden family in the Somerville affair of 1583. This would make sense in view of the satirizing of Falstaff himself as a Lollard. There is indeed something charming in the depiction of country life in these two scenes (iii.2 and v.1), but on closer attention to the meaning behind the words, we find our sinister impression of Falstaff only deepening.

Now it becomes inevitable that, once Prince Hal succeeds his father, Falstaff will be rejected. This is what takes place even in the new king's coronation procession, when Falstaff pushes himself forward expecting a welcome from the king, only to hear the painful words—painful to himself and all his fans—"I know thee not, old man. Fall to thy prayers!" (v.5). Now at last Falstaff is without Prince Hal: Prodigality without a prodigal son, and Waywardness without a wayward prince. In arithmetical terms, the fat old man is reduced to a zero, or nothing, without the thin 1 of the prince to support him. Yet in the Epilogue the poor dramatist is obliged to promise his eager spectators more of Falstaff in his next play of *Henry V* and to reassure the Protestant members of his audience—including the new Lord Chamberlain, Lord Cobham, Oldcastle's living descendant—that there is no connection between Sir John Falstaff and Sir John Oldcastle, "For Oldcastle died a martyr, and this is not the man." Such a barefaced disavowal, however, would have had only the opposite effect, to underline the connection (as subsequently recognized by Persons in his book *Of Three Conversions*). A further obligation incurred by the dramatist arose out of the queen's request to show "Falstaff in love," and so he had to compose his farce of *The Merry Wives of Windsor* almost entirely in prose. However, at this "Falstaff," without either Prince Hal or King Henry at his side, we can only exclaim, "This is not the man!"

That, however, isn't all there is to be said about Part II of *Henry IV*. For if there is an evident decline in the comic sub-plot with Falstaff and his friends, owing to the dwindling presence of Prince Hal, there is a corresponding rise in the element of tragedy in the main plot. From the outset there is a tragic accent in the frenzied words of Northumberland, as it were, in anticipation of Lear's madness: "Let heaven kiss earth! Now let not Nature's hand / Keep the wild flood con-fin'd! Let order die! / And let this world no longer be a stage / To feed contention in a lingering act!" (i.1). However, as before, at the time of his son Henry Hotspur's rebellion, so now, when it comes to decisive action, the old man finds it prudent—like his descendant at the time of the northern rebellion in 1569—to withdraw to Scotland (ii.3). In the same tragic vein, we have the speech of the aged king on his insomnia, reminding us of Macbeth's similar affliction: "How many thousand of my poorest subjects / Are at this hour asleep! O sleep! O gentle sleep! / Nature's soft nurse, how have I frighted thee!" (iii.1). In the same scene, he plaintively prays, "O God, that one might read the book of fate, / And see the revolution of the times / Make mountains level, and the continent— / Weary of solid firmness—melt itself / Into the sea!" Then in a similarly philosophical vein we hear Warwick's observation: "There is a history in all men's lives, / Figuring the nature of the times deceas'd." Even after the danger of rebellion has passed, the sense of tragedy remains in the dying moments of the king and his last words with the prince. First, we have the prince's reflections on the crown, so different from those of Richard of York and his son of Gloucester: "O polished perturbation! Golden care!" (iv.5). The ensuing conversation between him and his father lays emphasis not on the glory but on the heavy responsibil-ity of kingship. At the same time, the old king recurs to his original desire to lead a crusade to the Holy Land, but with so many rebellions on his hands he has been unable to keep his vow, till he dies in the chamber of his palace, appropriately named Jerusalem.

What a contrast is here—between the tragic accents of this main plot, with the newly established relations between king and prince, father and son, and the farce now requested by the aging queen to show "Falstaff in love"! At least there is more of the real Falstaff offstage in the seeming sequel of *Henry V.* Then, instead of keeping his promise to "continue the story, with Sir John in it," the dramatist merely narrates the dying words of Falstaff through the mouth of the tearful Dame Quickly, who assures her listeners that "he's in Arthur's bosom, if ever man went to Arthur's bosom"— though no man ever went to "Arthur's bosom" but only (in the words of Jesus, Luke xvi.22) to "Abraham's bosom"— adding that he also, like a very Puritan, "talked of the whore of Babylon." Here, the more we hear of Falstaff's end, with attention to the implications in his words, the more doubtful we become of his filmed representation by Sir Laurence Olivier. At least Olivier's performance is more Falstaffian than anything in *The Merry Wives of Windsor,* in which, for all his vaunted wit, Falstaff is unable to compete in wit with the merry wives.

chapter 6
Shylock

The Merchant of Venice

FROM TAMBURLAINE to the two Richards, of York and Gloucester, then from Edward II to the other Richard, of Bordeaux, and from Barabas to Shylock—it seems as if the shadow of the "dead shepherd" (as Marlowe is called in *As You Like It*, iii.5) is pursuing Shakespeare in his early efforts at dramatization, culminating in the last-named Jew. Scholars tend to fight shy of dealing with the question, "Why did Shakespeare write such and such a play?" since the answer usually has to be, "We don't know!" In this case, however, they aren't so shy. The year 1594 saw both the execution of the Jewish physician to the queen, Roderigo Lopez, on a charge of treason, and a revival of Marlowe's anti-Semitic play, *The Jew of Malta*. So it is commonly conjectured that Shakespeare was persuaded by his fellows in the newly formed Chamberlain's Men to cash in on the notoriety of the physician's execution and the popularity of Marlowe's drama with another play on a villainous Jew to be titled *The Merchant of Venice*. In his characterization of Shylock the Jew, however, Shakespeare is in no way indebted to Marlowe or his characterization of Barabas, whose melodramatic portrayal of a "Machiavel" is closer to Richard III.

From his first appearance in the third scene, as with that of Falstaff in the second scene of the first part of *Henry IV*, Shylock stands forth as a fully developed character. His medium of speech, like that of Falstaff, is more naturally prose than verse, except that in Shylock's case we may apply to him the Latin proverb *"Indignatio facit versum."* Rarely is Falstaff stirred by indignation to verse, but deep in the soul of Shylock we feel the fire of his and his people's indignation. From his opening words to Bassanio, on the proposed loan on the credit of the merchant Antonio, "Three thousand ducats, well. . . . For three months, well. . . . Antonio shall become bound, well . . . ," we may note the accents of worldly prudence and financial expertise in his voice. When, speaking as a Jew about his dealings with Christians, he adds, "I will buy with you, sell with you, talk with you, walk with you, and so following, but I will not eat with you, drink with you, nor pray with you," he still speaks in prose, yet there is a rhythmical rhetoric of emotion. Finally, on the entrance of Antonio, there is an impressive contrast between Shylock's opening aside, now at last in verse: "How like a fawning publican he looks! / I hate him for he is a Christian," and his set speech in reply to Antonio's offer: "Signior Antonio, many a time and oft / In the Rialto you have rated me / About my moneys and my usances."

Such is the portrayal of Shylock, not as a melodramatic villain like Barabas, but as a living human being, moved by a suppressed hatred and a lust for revenge. By contrast, the character of the merchant is weakly drawn, lacking in human color. It isn't surprising if many spectators or readers are left with the impression that the "merchant" of the title must be Shylock, not Antonio. From Antonio's opening words, "In sooth, I know not why I am so sad," we feel in him something pale and flaccid, yet mysterious. His friends go on to suggest one reason after another for his sadness, and critics of the play hasten to add reasons of their own drawn from Freudian psychology. In fact, as we are soon shown, it isn't so much care for his many ships with his merchandise on board as care for his friend Bassanio, who is now proposing to leave him on a pilgrimage to woo the lady Portia—such a familiar motive in Shakespeare's plays! It is in the hope of obtaining a loan to finance this journey that Bassanio now approaches Antonio, and as Antonio lacks the ready money, they go together to Shylock for this purpose. All the same, the mystery of Antonio remains from this beginning even till the end. Even when Bassanio wins the lady Portia, and his friend Gratiano wins her handmaid Nerissa, the "hero" of the play, Antonio, remains a bachelor, alone.

From this pair of friends, Antonio and Bassanio, and from the busy city of Venice—subsequently revisited by the dramatist in *Othello, the Moor of Venice*—we move to the ideal home of the lady Portia herself in Belmont, or "beautiful mountain." Yet from the beginning of this second scene, in which she is seen engaged in conversation with Nerissa, she caps the sadness of Antonio with a weariness of her own, as if foreshadowing that of a subsequent heroine, Rosalind in *As You Like It*. Portia is weary of her many suitors, who are drawn to her as much for her money as for her looks. She is also weary of her dead father's irksome condition, allowing her to marry only that suitor who makes the right choice out of three caskets—gold, silver, and lead. It is such a mysterious condition, corresponding to that other condition proposed by Shylock of a pound of flesh as pledge on the loan he is to offer Antonio. How Shakespeare seems to revel in such fairy-tale motifs, from his *Midsummer Night's Dream* to *The Tempest*, which paradoxically serve to bring out the humanity of his characters, their words and actions!

All he requires of his spectators and readers is a willing sus-pension of disbelief.

Out of these parallel plots, involving first Bassanio and next Antonio, the dramatist skillfully leads to two climactic scenes, first of the choice and next of the trial. In the choice of Bassanio, after two other suitors have made theirs—the Prince of Morocco, his choice of gold, and the Prince of Arragon, his choice of silver—all emphasis is laid on the speech in which he deliberates before he chooses, according to the proverb "look before you leap." In his speech, he states the "moral" implicit in all Shakespeare's plays, in spite of the reluctance of scholars to regard the dramatist as a moralist: "So may the outward shows be least themselves. / The world is still deceiv'd with ornament." So he is prompted to make his choice of the "meager lead," saying, "Thy plainness moves me more than eloquence" (iii.1). Nat-urally, according to Shakespeare's logic, he wins the hand of Portia. It is all very simple, with such a happy ending—until all is changed by a word from Antonio in Venice, that his sea ventures have failed, that he is unable to repay the loan, that he is now at the mercy of Shylock, and that Shylock is insisting on legal justice.

The play moves back from Belmont to Venice and from the casket scene to the trial scene. Shylock is now so sure of winning his case that he is already preparing the knife to cut off a pound of Antonio's flesh nearest to his heart. None of those present, not even Bassanio with promises of twice the sum in repayment, can move him with their pleas for mercy, until Portia enters disguised as a lawyer. Then, after seeming to recognize the justice of Shylock's position, she comes out with her celebrated plea for mercy, beginning, "The quality of mercy is not strain'd. / It droppeth as the gentle rain from heaven / Upon the place beneath" (iv.1). Even so, Shylock is adamant on taking his stand by the law and is about to exact his pledge from Antonio when Portia stays his hand, changing her tactics from mercy to justice. Now in a neat turning of the tables against him, she herself appeals to certain laws of Venice that have hitherto been overlooked. Shylock is now defeated, he has no answer, and he withdraws from the court in confusion. But first, in accumulation of humiliation, he is obliged by the court to renounce his Judaism and to receive Christian baptism, though contrary to human justice and Christian practice.

Still, for the Christians it is a happy outcome. They forget about poor Shylock, who has now lost both his Jewish identity and his precious ducats, as well as his daughter Jessica, who has run away from home with the Christian Lorenzo and herself received baptism. They all gather again in Belmont to celebrate their triumph, if with a humorous trick played by Portia and Nerissa (in their former disguises as lawyer and lawyer's clerk) on their newly wed husbands, Bassanio and Gratiano, when all they will take for their services are the rings they notice on the fingers of those two, though they have sworn never to part with them. It is an odd triviality with which to end a play, but it is overshadowed by the ideal imagery of "the music of the spheres" with its heavenly harmony, introduced by the lovers Lorenzo and Jessica (who have been left at Belmont in Portia's absence). It is also followed by good news for Antonio of the safe return of all his ships to harbor. In this way light rises out of darkness and new life out of seeming death.

This all remains, however—despite the skilful development of the intertwined plots, the brilliant portrayal of human character, and the memorable poetry in such speeches as those of Bassanio and Portia—on the level of outward appearances. And it is with such appearances, as Bassanio (and Shakespeare in him) is careful to remind us, that the world of Shakespearian scholarship is still deceived. For beneath the seeming secularism of the play one can hardly help noticing the underlying vein of religious and biblical reference. Here it is less disguised than usual, as the subject itself implies the traditional division reaching back to biblical times between Jew and Christian, the Old Law and the New Law, the ideals of justice and mercy. It is only natural for Shakespeare to characterize the Jew with utterances drawn from the Old Testament, considering that his knowledge of Jews must needs come rather from the Bible than from personal acquaintance. Even so, it is interesting to note how many of Shylock's biblical utterances are derived as much from the New as from the Old Testament. He is indeed more religious and biblical in his speech than almost any of the Christians, apart from Antonio and Portia. At the climax of the play in the trial scene, one may well be impressed by the extent of the play's biblical reference, not least in Portia's plea for mercy—beginning with the imagery of rain, which is a symbol of the divine Word in the Old Testament and of God's fatherly providence in Christ's Sermon on the Mount.

It seems as if, in spite of the almost universal disapproval of secular scholars, Shakespeare is revealing himself in this play in his true colors, as preacher no less than playwright. It may be his professed aim to entertain his audiences and to make a living for himself and his fellow actors of the Chamberlain's Men. But his was no modern "art for art's sake," with art divorced from morality. In this at least he fully conformed to the critical ideal of the Renaissance, that entertainment should be combined with instruction. Only, his idea of instruction went beyond both the Bible and the commonplaces of morality. In this as in his other plays, or even more than in his other plays, he looked to the particular religious situation in England. On the one hand, in his characterization of Shylock, he shows us not just a Jew, of whom he could have known very few outside the pages of the Bible, but a Christian Jew, as the Puritans of his time were called because of their imitation of biblical manners and their choice of biblical names for their children. The Puritans in England were strict in their dealings with others, many of whom they regarded as little better than heathen. Like the Jews in other countries, they often engaged in lending money at usurious rates of interest, according to the accusation leveled against their leader Thomas Cartwright by his Anglican critic, Matthew Sutcliffe. Thus in Shylock's Venice, as in Ephesus in *The Comedy of Errors*, we may see a reflection of Shakespeare's London.

Now, if Shylock is seen in contemporary terms as a Puritan, how may we regard his adversaries, Antonio and Bassanio, if not as Catholics? In particular, we note how Antonio is from the outset helping his friend Bassanio go on a "pilgrimage" to the lady of his dreams across the sea to Belmont—a situation we have already noted in *The Two Gentlemen of Verona* and *The Taming of the Shrew*. As noted above, it was also the situation in Elizabethan England from the time of Shakespeare's boyhood, when Catholic priests like Campion and Persons were concerned not only to provide for the spiritual needs of their fellow countrymen but also to send suitable young men for their Catholic education abroad in one or other of the seminaries. This may well be the enigma behind Antonio's sadness at the beginning of the play, seeing that (as Bassanio attests) he is "one in whom / The ancient Roman honour more appears / Than any that draws breath in Italy" (iii.2). As for Bassanio's motive, he is drawn to the lady Portia as (in Morocco's words) "this shrine, this mortal-breathing saint" (ii.7). He regards her in much the same way as Proteus regarded Silvia, and Romeo regarded Juliet, in terms of the Virgin Mary.

Portia herself is not exactly spoken of in terms of "grace," like the other heroines. But her feminine ideal is praised by Shylock's runaway daughter Jessica, who says of Bassanio that "having such a blessing in his lady, / He finds his joys of heaven here on earth" and that "the poor rude world / Hath not her fellow" (iii.5). Being Italian, Portia is naturally presented by the dramatist as Catholic, only she is more devout than most of her countrymen. Thus she explains her absence from Belmont in going to Venice: "I have toward heaven breath'd a secret vow / To live in prayer and contemplation" at "a monastery two miles off" (iii.3). Then on her return home she is said to have been straying about "by holy crosses, where she kneels and prays / For happy wedlock hours" (v.1). These may be lies, but they are white, even devout, lies, not without an element of symbolic truth in them. As for the name of her home, this, too, would have had a Catholic ring in the dramatist's ears, since a cousin of his noble patron, the Earl of Southampton, was Thomas Pounde of Belmont (a place in Hampshire). Pounde had spent years in prison as a Catholic recusant and had been instrumental in disseminating Campion's Brag, or "Letter to the Lords of the Council," in 1580, being admitted to the Society of Jesus while still in prison.

Finally, it may be added that the duet of the lovers Lorenzo and Jessica with which Act V opens, while openly referring to such classical personages as Troilus and Cressida, Pyramus and Thisbe, Dido and Aeneas, Jason and Medea, contains a hidden echo of the Catholic liturgy for the Easter Vigil, with its theme of new life rising out of the night of death. In stanza upon stanza the lovers begin with the

words, "In such a night as this," as it were, echoing the repetition of the Latin *"Haec nox est"*—This is the night—from
the solemn hymn sung by the deacon after the blessing of
the fire, *"Exultet iam angelica turba caelorum"*—Now let the
angelic host of heaven exult. (The same hymn is, it may be
added, also recalled by the holy old man Gonzalo, in pro-
nouncing his blessing on another pair of lovers, Ferdinand
and Miranda, in the happy ending of *The Tempest*.) Lorenzo
also goes on to speak in Christian Platonic terms of "the
sounds of music" and "sweet harmony," with reference to
each star in the sky that "like an angel sings, / Still quiring
to the young-eyed cherubins." This serves to prepare us for
the entrance of the lady Portia, while it is still night, as from
a distance she sees a light burning in her hall. Then she
wonders "how far that little candle throws his beams," with
the moral, "So shines a good deed in a naughty world"—
echoing Christ's words, "Let your light so shine before men,
that they may see your good works and glorify your Father
who is in heaven" (Matt v.16). There, Shakespeare would
surely agree, is at once the meaning and the moral of *The
Merchant of Venice*, with all respect to those who would deny
any such moral, while mistakenly pleading the cause of Shylock, whether as Jew or Puritan.

chapter 7
Another
Annus Mirabilis

As You Like It

IN THE YEAR 1599, with the opening of the new Globe
Theatre on the South Bank of the Thames, Shakespeare
seems to have celebrated yet another *annus mirabilis* with the
composition and production of three more plays straddling
the three genres of comedy, history, and tragedy. The comedy *As You Like It* appears as the most genial of his "happy
comedies" (according to the grouping made by J. Dover
Wilson in 1962), with its evocation of Shakespeare's old
home in the Forest of Arden, and its memorable speech put
into the mouth of the melancholy Jaques, "All the world's a
stage" (ii.7). This is interpreted as the dramatist's rendering
of the Latin motto for the new theatre from Petronius,
"Totus mundus agit histrionem"—All the world plays the
player. The history is the last in Shakespeare's series of plays
from English history (apart from his last-minute collaboration in *Henry VIII*), the seemingly "patriotic" play of *Henry
V*, with an opening Chorus celebrating "this wooden O" or
Globe, on whose "unworthy scaffold" is commemorated the
famous victory of Henry at Agincourt. The tragedy is the
first of the Roman plays, *Julius Caesar*, in which at the very
moment of Caesar's assassination the murderer Cassius is

sufficiently aware of his theatrical surroundings to exclaim, "How many ages hence / Shall this our lofty scene be acted o'er, / In states unborn and accents yet unknown!" (iii.1).

Turning back to the comedy of *As You Like It*, we may note how typically—as in *The Comedy of Errors* and *A Midsummer Night's Dream*—the drama opens with a cloud of tragedy in both settings. At the ducal court, the old duke (identified only as Duke Senior) has been displaced by his usurping younger brother, while he himself has been banished to the Forest of Arden. At the home of the brothers de Boys, the younger Orlando has been kept from his rightful inheritance by his elder brother Oliver. Thus, as also in the subsequent plays of *Hamlet*, *King Lear*, and *The Tempest*, we have the typical biblical situation of two brothers, like Cain and Abel, present in the background even of comedy. The immediate outcome is not death but banishment in either case to the Forest of Arden, with the result that, as in *King Lear*, we find all the good characters moving from court and city to the forest.

As for the location of this forest, it was no doubt for the dramatist himself his native Forest of Arden, whose memory is in many ways present throughout the play. In Shakespeare's dramatic source, however, Thomas Lodge's pastoral romance of *Rosalynde*, the setting was a forest in France vaguely located somewhere between Bordeaux and Lyons, seemingly by mistake for the historic mountain-forest of the Ardennes on the border between France and the Low Countries. As this latter forest included within its domain the town of Douai, with the English seminary under Dr. William Allen, it is not unlikely that Shakespeare, with his Catholic sympathies, also had this place in mind. From his boyhood he had been accustomed to a connection between the two forests, with so many young men (such as his school friend from Shottery, Robert Dibdale, who accompanied his master Simon Hunt to Douai in 1575) going abroad for their studies at the seminary. Nor is it unlikely that the exiled duke might have stood for Dr. Allen himself, considering the description of the duke in exile given by Charles the wrestler in the opening scene. There we hear of "three or four loving lords" who "have put themselves into voluntary exile with him" (such as Thomas Houghton, the elder brother of Alexander, who went into exile in 1569 to help Allen with his foundation), while "many young gentlemen flock to him every day" (such as the young seminarians, many of whom came from "gentle" families). There is even something nostalgic about the situation of such exiles, who "live like the old Robin Hood of England" and "fleet the time carelessly, as they did in the golden world" (i.1). The heroine Rosalind, daughter to the exiled duke, also goes into exile with her cousin Celia, though daughter to the usurping duke, in the conviction—similar to that later affirmed by Kent in *King Lear* (i.1)—"Now go we in content / To liberty and not to banishment" (i.3).

From Act II we leave the court and the city (if Orlando's house is in the city, though its location, too, is obscure) behind and enter the Forest of Arden, where the new setting is introduced to us by the exiled duke himself. His speech is indeed a kind of sermon, based on the popular Christian classic by Thomas à Kempis, *The Imitation of Christ*, on "the uses of adversity" (bk. I, ch. xii). The duke's speech culminates in the monastic ideal, which had no doubt been shared by the nuns of Wroxhall Abbey: "And this our life, exempt from public haunt, / Finds tongues in trees, books in the running brooks, / Sermons in stones, and good in everything" (ii.1). Those "sermons in stones" might even refer to the ruined stones of the abbey. The same nostalgia recurs in Orlando's challenge, on his arrival in Arden, to those who "under the shade of melancholy boughs" seem "to lose and neglect the creeping hours of time" by recalling those "better days" when "bells have knoll'd to church" (ii.7). No longer, it seems, can they enjoy the comforts of what Hamlet calls "sweet religion" (*Hamlet* iii.4).

All the same, in the course of a play where nothing special happens apart from love affairs, it is surprising to find so many religious men of one kind or another in or around the forest. The only one with a name is Sir Oliver Martext, evidently a Puritan minister (from the association of his name with the Puritan Martin Marprelate, who flourished even in Warwickshire in the aftermath of the Armada), but his offered ministrations to one pair of lovers, Touchstone and Audrey, are spurned by the melancholy Jaques, one of the exiled lords, and so presumably a Catholic (iii.3). Then there is the unnamed uncle of Rosalind, who has provided her with a remedy against love and who is reported by Orlando to be living "[o]bscured in the circle of this forest" (v.4). There is also the "old religious man," who meets the usurping duke on the latter's way to the forest to apprehend his brother, and who by means of a single conversation converts him from his dukedom to a retired religious life (v.4). Evidently there is a kindly religious spell at work in the forest, enabling the residents to "find good in everything."

In such a forest the quality of "grace" is to be found, needless to say, in the heroine Rosalind, even though she has assumed male attire for the purpose of self-protection. Her description comes from the pen of her lover Orlando, who isn't aware of her proximity. In a poem he has affixed to a tree in the forest he writes of her: "Therefore heaven Nature charg'd / That one body should be fill'd / With all graces wide enlarg'd" (iii.2). We also hear the idealistic shepherd lover Silvius, who speaks of himself in relation to his love for the shepherdess Phoebe: "So holy and so perfect is my love, / And I in such a poverty of grace," regarding Phoebe (an alternative name for the goddess Diana) as the source of his grace (iii.5). It is Rosalind who is the source of all the good that comes to the characters, not least of all to the lovers, in this play. It is also she who effectively presides, rather than the masked figure named Hymen, over the engagement ceremony at the end, with its opening echo of Christ's words, "Then is there mirth in heaven, / When earthly things made even / Atone together" (v.4, cf. Luke xv.7,10).

Such is the simple pastoral play with the odd title of *As You Like It*, which anticipates the alternative title of *Twelfth Night*, namely *What You Will*. It seems an off-putting title, as if the dramatist couldn't be bothered to give his play a suitable title, so when asked by the manager for a title, he merely replied, "You can call it as you like it." And so the play was accordingly titled *As You Like It*. All the same, audiences have ever since liked the play, which has become one of the most popular of Shakespeare's comedies, with its nostalgia for country life in "merry England."

Henry V

The next play of 1599, with its opening mention of "this wooden O," is the last of the English history plays, *Henry V*. In some respects it is often seen as the last of the "second tetralogy" of those plays, or at least as the last of the three Falstaff plays that have been grouped as a trilogy. But in other respects, more intrinsic to the play itself, it has to stand by itself alone, in contrast as well to the preceding Falstaff plays as to all the other plays of English history. In it the dramatist barefacedly breaks his promise, made in the Epilogue to Part II of *Henry IV*, to "continue the story, with Sir John in it." For

Sir John conspicuously fails to appear, except in the description of his dying moments by Dame Quickly. His companions may appear, with the swaggering Pistol and the newly invented Nym with his passion for "humour" (in his unique meaning of the word), and in them his presence is somehow perpetuated. But he himself is no longer there. Then without him to provide the necessary zero, as noted above, the 10 of Prince Hal as prodigal son is reduced to a narrow 1 as King Henry. For all his ranting, as patriotically exaggerated by Sir Laurence Olivier in the film version, the king is only a shadow of the prince, and the prince is only himself with Falstaff at his side. So there is something essentially unpopular about the play, as proved by the scarcity of its performances.

Shakespeare himself could hardly have been unaware of this human deficiency in his hero, nor yet was he unaware of the possibility of irony in taking him as the central figure of this last of his plays on English history. King Henry is alone, as a narrow 1 without the necessary zero of Falstaff, but at least in place of Falstaff Shakespeare bolsters the figure of his hero with an alternative zero in the form of an enthusiastic Chorus. Needless to say, as victor of Agincourt, with which he brought the Hundred Years' War to a triumphant close, Henry was not without appeal to a certain Protestant patriotism in the Elizabethan audience, and it is on this patriotism that the Chorus plays from act to act, as a kind of cheerleader to make up for what is lacking in the performance of the army commander. So in the end—whose happy outcome in a projected marriage is undercut by the sad Epilogue—the one character who stands out most impressively in our minds is not so much the commander as the cheerleader, this one-man Chorus with the audience as his hoped-for choir.

The insufficiency of Henry as newly enthroned king is apparent from the outset, for all the praise of his prelates, who speak of him (though male) as "full of grace and fair regard" and who applaud his unexpected "reformation" as effected "with such a heady currance, scouring faults." The historical period may have been Catholic, but the prelates, with their conviction that "miracles are ceas'd," are clearly Anglican, considering that such was the Anglican position in contemporary controversies with the Catholics. Moreover, in the next scene they are shown as abject flatterers of the king, supporting his devious claim to the throne of France and justifying his plans of war. Speciously, the king may charge them on their "conscience" to declare nothing but the truth, but from the circumstances of self-interest on either side it is sufficiently clear that "truth" is but a synonym for flattery. On the one hand, the king's mind is already made up to go to war, not only in pursuance of a doubtful claim to the French throne, but also in order to distract the minds of his nobles from the weakness of his own claim to the throne of England. On the other hand, it is in the mind of the bishops to distract the minds of both rulers and people from a proposal to pillage the lands of the Church. In this new alliance between Church and state, we notice in the new king a change in character from Prince Hal to King Henry, as he has put his prodigality (in the person of Falstaff) on one side and adopted an appearance of religious piety, similar to that for which his youthful successor Henry VI came to be famous. Yet there remains an underlying continuity of Machiavellian policy aptly expressed in the word "hypocrisy." In his days as Prince Hal, he could remain secular, with hardly a trace of religious feeling, since his hypocrisy was sufficiently personified in Falstaff, but now as King Henry it is incumbent on him, being no less Machiavellian than Richard III or Iago, to "show out a flag and sign" of piety (*Othello* i.1). Such is after all the explicit recommendation of Machiavelli in *The Prince*.

Now at last, with Falstaff easily disposed of in Dame Quickly's affecting account of his end, we follow King Henry with his army to France and see him haranguing his troops before the gates of Harfleur. There he makes his "fascist" appeal to the patriotic emotions of both his English soldiers and his Elizabethan audience in words made famous by Sir Laurence Olivier: "Once more into the breach, dear friends, once more!" (They are so much more famous than their ominous sequel: "Or close the wall up with our English dead!" [iii.1].) No less than Macbeth, Henry is a man of blood, not caring whether the blood he sheds is that of friend or foe. He confesses, "In peace there's nothing so becomes a man / As modest stillness and humility"—so long as all is done in due subjection to himself as king, however weak may be his claims to the throne. But, he continues, "when the blast of war blows in our ears, / Then imitate the action of a tiger." Nor is that all in the way of English fascism, but in a subsequent scene he goes on to utter the direst threats against the citizens of Harfleur, warning them of what will befall them if they fail to admit him and his army. For then, he declares, "The gates of mercy shall be all shut up," and then his soldiers "in liberty of bloody hand shall range / With conscience wide as hell, mowing like grass / Your fresh-fair virgins and your flowering infants," even, he dares to add, like "Herod's bloody-hunting slaughtermen" (iii.3). Indeed, "the war-like Harry," as he is admiringly described by the toady Chorus, has come to appear in prophetic anticipation no less a ranter than Adolf Hitler.

The real climax of the play, however, is to be found not so much in this pseudopatriotic, jingoistic speechifying, as in what a subsequent Chorus (to Act IV) sycophantically describes as "a little touch of Harry in the night." Here we have an impressive scene in which the king humbly confesses, "I think the king is but a man as I am. The violet smells to him as it doth to me," and so on (iv.1). It is indeed very touching, and it may remind us of Prince Hal when he confesses in *Henry IV*, Part I, "I am now of all humours that have show'd themselves humours since the old days of goodman Adam" (ii.4), and of Shylock, too, "I am a Jew. Hath not a Jew eyes," and so on (iii.1). After all, is it enough to put on the airs of humanity and humility when a man will not face the harsh truth about himself? But that is what the common soldier, in the person of the young Michael Williams, goes on to show the king under the cover of darkness and disguise. The king may insist that his cause is just and his quarrel honorable, as certified by the flattering prelates. But, answers Williams, "That's more than we know." After all, "If the cause be not good, the king himself hath a heavy reckoning to make, when all those legs and arms and heads, chopped off in a battle, shall join together at the latter day, and cry all, 'We died at such a place.' " It is an eloquent argument, put by the dramatist into the mouth of the common man, for peace and against war, especially against such a war as the king is now waging in France. This is what the king himself subsequently admits, when he goes on to say in soliloquy: "Not today, O Lord! / O not today, think not upon the fault / My father made in compassing the crown." Now at last, thanks to the frank words of the common soldier, King Henry comes to recognize the weakness of his position, not only on the field of battle where his forces are outnumbered by the French, but also in himself. Nor can he hope to buy the divine approval by building chantry chapels "for Richard's soul," when he well knows (like Claudius in his corresponding soliloquy in *Hamlet* iii.3), "All I can do is nothing worth, / Since that my penitence comes after all, / Imploring pardon." He may go on to win a notable victory over the French numbers at Agincourt, but that is nothing compared to this fleeting moment of sincerity that gleams amidst the dark clouds of his religious hypocrisy. At this moment he may be compared to that other Machiavellian, Richard III, in his flash of sincere soliloquy on the eve of Bosworth. Yet, as St. Ignatius keenly shows in his meditation on Three Classes of Men in *The Spiritual Exercises* (a passage that was no doubt in Shakespeare's mind both here and in *Hamlet*), such a moment isn't enough for true repentance when unaccompanied by answering deeds of satisfaction.

Yet another unique aspect of this play, in which the dramatist has prudently broken his promise to the people in denying them a return to the old rogue, Sir John Falstaff (killing him off instead), is his addition of another inimitable character by the side of the new king. This is a comic character of Welsh origin—whom the old Falstaff might well have despised, in the words of his namesake in *The Merry Wives of Windsor*, as "one that makes fritters of English" (v.5)—namely Fluellen. He is in his own conceit a master in the ancient art of warfare, especially the old classical warfare, and so he can't help admiring King Henry as a reincarnation of Alexander the Great, or "Alexander the Pig," as he names him, in a Welsh rendering of "Big" (iv.7). Endowed as he is with such a Welsh pronunciation of English, he is also a master comedian—just as English or Japanese comedians win an easy fame by imitating the northern pronunciation of their language. Indeed, but for the fact of his having been preceded on the stage by Sir John Falstaff (and that other Welshman, the parson Sir Hugh Evans), he might well have ranked among Shakespeare's great comic creations. Above all, in his panoramic view of world history, he has a charmingly mediaeval tendency to find "figures in all things," even when there is an obvious inconsistency in his choice of "figures and comparisons" (iv.7). He champions Henry against Alexander, even in the king's rejection of "the fat knight with the great belly-doublet," whose name Fluellen has amusingly forgotten.

Finally, if only to show that this is more than a merely "patriotic play," but a comedy with the required happy ending—an ending that has to take the form not of victory in battle but of marriage—Shakespeare adds a long prosaic scene of Henry's wooing of princess Katharine. Here in contrast to his warlike rhetoric at the Siege of Harfleur, and his poetic meditations on "ceremony" and "the crown" on the eve of Agincourt, Henry introduces himself to his would-be bride (still, one can't help thinking, with his customary hypocrisy) as "a fellow of plain and uncoined constancy" (v.2). His medium may now be prose, but he reveals himself as one of those whom he contemptuously calls "fellows of infinite tongue, that can rime themselves into ladies' favours" at considerable length and with considerable eloquence. At the same time, we know that it is all unnecessary, as Katharine has already been schooled by her parents into accepting the royal proposal whether made in verse or in prose. So for the time being, the outcome is peace, according to the prayer of the French queen Isabella: "God, the best maker of all marriages, / Combine your hearts in one, your realms in one!" Only, alas, the eventual outcome is the untimely death of King Henry and the accession of his pious son, another King Henry, with a renewal of war in France, then also in England—as recalled in the now subdued words of the Chorus, who at last has to face the unpleasant truth, "which oft our stage hath shown" in the three tedious parts of *Henry VI*.

▇ *Julius Caesar*

In the same admirable year of 1599 we move from the last of the English history plays, *Henry V*—always excepting

Shakespeare's collaboration in *Henry VIII*—to the first of the Roman plays, *Julius Caesar*. This is, however, counted not as a history play, nor yet as a Roman play, but as a tragedy—in the same way as *Titus Andronicus* and *Romeo and Juliet* are counted as tragedies, on account of their sad endings. Yet, as I insist, each play is unique, as when the villain Richard of Gloucester says of himself in *Henry VI*, Part III, "I am myself alone" (v.6). To give each of these plays its due: *Titus Andronicus* is a dramatic parody of the old revenge play; *Romeo and Juliet* is a romantic comedy that changes by accident or fate into a tragedy; but *Julius Caesar*, centered as it is on the assassination of Julius Caesar (according to the altered title chosen by Charlton Heston for his film version), is a pure tragedy—one of the purest tragedies Shakespeare ever wrote. Not that Caesar is the hero in his own play. He is just the figure at the center of the action, but he is without any interiority. He is all outside, a very caricature of himself, what with his defects of hearing, his superstitious fears, his boastfulness, and his inconstancy even when proclaiming, "I am as constant as the Northern star" (iii.1). No, the real hero is his assassin, his friend and reputed son, Brutus, whose interiority is emphasized from the outset as the target of temptation by the quasi-villain Cassius.

This tragedy is, moreover, noteworthy for the abundant use of rhetoric, which at once distinguishes it from all other plays by Shakespeare and makes it truly Roman (more than the other so-called Roman plays), according to the ideal of the great Roman orator Cicero, who himself plays a minor role in it. From the outset we have the rhetorical appeal of the tribune Marullus to the people of Rome, with a generous use of triplets that are both impressive in their studied eloquence and ineffective in winning over the hearts of the Romans. The same eloquence is soon to be found on the lips of Cassius in his temptation of Brutus, beginning with "I was born free as Caesar, so were you" and culminating with "Ye gods, it doth amaze me, / A man of such a feeble temper should / So get the start of the majestic world, / And bear the palm alone" (i.2). Only Cassius is too clever to antagonize Brutus as Marullus has antagonized the Romans. He prudently leaves Brutus to think about what he has said and to indulge in his propensity to soliloquize, so that the outcome may seem to come not from any browbeating on his part but from his friend's own decision. So when Brutus turns, like Hamlet, to reflection, he says, "It must be by his death"—typically stating his conclusion before having considered any arguments. Yet he is also like Macbeth in his feeling of horror at what he is about to do, when he goes on to reflect, "Between the acting of a dreadful thing / And the first motion, all the interim is / Like a phantasma, or a hideous dream" (ii.1).

It is only later, when Brutus and Cassius have (in Macbeth's words) "done the deed" (ii.2) and Caesar is dead, that Cassius looks forward to the future—interestingly, in terms of the outcome not of his and Brutus's enterprise but of their theatrical fame: "How many ages hence / Shall this our lofty scene be acted o'er, / In states unborn and accents yet unknown!" (iii.1). Then we hear two more rhetorical speeches, one by Brutus in prose, in defense of what they have done, and the other by Mark Antony in verse, in memory of his friend Caesar, but implicitly against Caesar's assassins. The words of Brutus are carefully measured, weighed on the scales of reason and formulated in the rhetorical tradition of Rome. For a time he succeeds in persuading his hearers of the justice of his cause, to such an extent that they paradoxically vote to make him Caesar in place of the man he has just assassinated for his ambition. Then, almost at once, with the approval of Brutus, Antony

begins his speech with the more insidious eloquence of
verse, and the opening triplet, "Friends, Romans, countrymen!" Then with ever-mounting eloquence he wins over
the hearts, as well as the minds, of the Romans, till they are
ready to rush forth and burn the houses of the conspirators.
Finally, once his words have had their effect, Antony stands
back with the sinister remark, "Now let it work! Mischief,
thou art afoot, / Take thou what course thou wilt!" (iii.2)—
anticipating the no-less-sinister words of Iago in *Othello*,
"Work on, / My medicine, work!" (iv.1).

Reflecting on the impact of rhetoric on the human mind,
as Shakespeare shows us in this play, we can't help recognizing that we, too, no less than the citizens of Rome, are members of the audience. How easily we are swayed by the power
of words, whether of Brutus or Antony, whether of Hitler or
Mussolini, whether even of the serpent to Eve in the Garden
of Eden—as Milton also noted in his account of the temptation of Eve in Book VIII of *Paradise Lost*, "As when of old
some orator renowned / In Athens or free Rome, where eloquence / Flourished." In this connection it is often asked, on
which side does the dramatist take his stand, that of Caesar
and Antony, or that of the assassins, Brutus and Cassius? It is
the same question as that asked concerning *Richard II*,
whether he sides with Bolingbroke or Richard. Of the latter
play it may be said that Shakespeare evidently sides with
whichever of the two happens to be the underdog, and so he
sympathizes with Bolingbroke when he has to "tread the
stranger paths of banishment" (i.3), and later with Richard
when he goes to prison. In *Julius Caesar*, however, it may be
said that he shows up the weaknesses of both sides, not only
the infirmity of Caesar and the ambition of Antony, but also
the envy of Cassius and the foolish idealism of Brutus. Yet
insofar as he sides with anyone in the play, it is Brutus

whom he finally commends, in the generous eulogy of Antony: "His life was gentle, and the elements / So mix'd in him that Nature might stand up / And say to all the world, 'This was a man!' " (v.5). Not that Shakespeare approves of the actions of Brutus, still less of the flawed logic behind those actions. Rather, he shows Brutus deciding to kill Caesar before having duly weighed the reasons for and against the deed. Even in presenting the reasons, with the words, "Fashion it thus," he shows the hero shamelessly twisting the reasons into conformity with his conclusion (ii.1).

As for the second half of the play, once Caesar has been assassinated, and the speeches of Brutus and Antony are over, and Brutus and Cassius have fled from Rome, all that follows is a long drawn-out anticlimax. Act IV is occupied with the episode of the quarrel between Brutus and Cassius, and Act V with their defeat by the forces of Antony and Octavius at the battle of Philippi, but the real interest of the audience is already over by the end of Act III. Now what Brutus observes to Cassius, once they have patched up their quarrel, ironically applies to himself and his part in the play: "There is a tide in the affairs of men, / Which taken at the flood leads on to fortune, / Omitted, all the voyage of their life / Is bound in shallows and in miseries" (iv.3). Maybe he was endeavoring to take the tide at the flood with the assassination of Julius Caesar, but his seeming success was turned into real failure by the one speech of Antony. All the same, one may add that in his failure Brutus has paradoxically been more successful in winning audiences to the play of *Julius Caesar* than King Henry was in his victory over the French at the battle of Agincourt—for all the support of Sir Laurence Olivier in his patriotic film version of *Henry V*.

chapter 8
The Comedian

▦ Trifling Titles

THERE IS no doubt that Shakespeare had a soft spot in his heart for fools like Bottom, rogues like Falstaff, and even villains like Shylock. What these fools, rogues, and villains have in common is a certain touch of humanity, which is brought out by their folly, their roguery, and even their villainy. Thus the folly of Bottom achieves an inverted climax in what he names "Bottom's Dream," his vision of love-making with the fairy queen Titania (*A Midsummer Night's Dream* iv.1). The roguery of Falstaff comes to a similarly inverted climax in his outrageous "catechism of honour" on the battlefield of Shrewsbury (*Henry IV*, Part I, v.1). Even the villainy of Shylock is softened, attenuated, and palliated by his self-justification of revenge, "Hath not a Jew eyes?" and so on (*The Merchant of Venice* iii.1). In the same way, if we may take a leap forward into the reign of James I and the play *The Winter's Tale*, it seems as if Shakespeare had an even softer spot in his heart for petty thieves like Autolycus, who professes to be (like his creator) "a snapper-up of unconsidered trifles" (iv.2).

It may indeed be said of all Shakespeare's plays that they are, as it were, quilts or patchworks of such "unconsidered trifles." Robert Greene spoke truly of him, if with some professional rancor, in denouncing him and his plays as dressed in borrowed feathers, not a few of them purloined from the work of Greene himself and other university wits. That was Greene writing in 1592, on the very eve of his death, long before he could have seen the full extent of Shakespeare's thievery. It was only centuries later that Richard Farmer, in his essay "On the Learning of Shakespeare" (1767), came to the conclusion that "all such reading as was never read is the reading necessary for a comment on Shakespeare." Indeed, Shakespeare was never particular about his sources. He had no snobbish nose for what Matthew Arnold commended as "the best that is known and thought in the world" (*Essays in Criticism*, 1865). Rather, Shakespeare was interested (like G. K. Chesterton) in the penny dreadfuls of his age, in the cheap popular ballads, in all that strikes us as inferior from a literary or artistic or Eliotic viewpoint.

This all leads, strange as it may seem, to a consideration of the mature comedies that follow on *The Merchant of Venice* while remaining within the limits of the Elizabethan age. One of them, *As You Like It*, we have already considered as providing the *annus mirabilis* of 1599 with the element of comedy. The title of the play is so trifling, so nonchalant, so off-putting, as if to say, "Take it or leave it!" or "Call it what you like, but don't trouble me!" Then there is *Much Ado About Nothing*, whose title betrays much the same mood of nonchalance, as if to say, "Really, there's nothing special about this play. The plot may seem to be intricate and ingenious, but there's nothing to it. Or if there is anything, it is to be found not so much in 'nothing' as in 'noting,' whether in the sense of 'spying,' observing while remaining unobserved, or of singing or playing notes." And then there is *Twelfth Night*, with its alternative title *What You Will*, which sounds like another way of saying "As you like it," with an additional pun on the poet's name (as in his "Will" sonnets). As for the main title, it refers not so much to anything in the play (save to the minds of ingenious critics) as to the date on which the play was first performed, the twelfth night after Christmas, or more precisely (according to the convincing theory of Leslie Hotson in *The First Night of Twelfth Night*, 1954) the evening of January 6, 1601—the last night of the Christmas festivities at court and a feast of fools.

Why then, it may be asked, did Shakespeare hit upon such trivial titles for these three mature comedies of his, which are commonly dated around the turn of the century? Is it that he couldn't be bothered to think of any more appropriate titles for them? Or is it that he considered, once he had got the text of the play off his hands, he might safely leave the choice of a title to the stage manager, as a modern author is often obliged to leave the choice of a title for his book to the whim of the publisher? Or is it, as we find Claudius suspecting of Hamlet, after having overheard the staged conversation between him and Ophelia, that "there's something in his soul / O'er which his melancholy sits on brood"? (*Hamlet* iii.1).

In my opinion, the last-mentioned suggestion comes closest to the truth, as we have to deal with a dramatist whose mind is inexorably moving into the final, storm-tossed years of the Elizabethan age. It is as if everything in his dramatic genius is crying out for something tragic, something in accord with his deepest feelings. Only, for the time being, he has to bow to public demand, as he has always done, and to satisfy the people with "a sop to Cerberus," that many-headed monster. So he churns out this series of comedies, tossing them off as "unconsidered trifles" while putting into each a pinch of tragic content. In their composition he hardly seems to take the trouble (as Ben Jonson noted of him) to blot a line or (as Dr. Samuel Johnson remarked of his plays) to devise a convenient conclusion, still less to provide them with a suitable title.

■ *Much Ado About Nothing*

The first thing to be noticed about *Much Ado About Nothing* is that in touching on his favorite theme of "nothing," as if echoing the words of the imprisoned king in *Richard II* (v.5), the dramatist now elevates that theme to the status of his chosen title. The play may be regarded as a play (in both senses of the word "play") on "nothing." But then, we may ask, what precisely is the "nothing" about which "much ado" is said to be made in the play? Or alternatively, what precisely is the "much ado" about which nothing is made? Such questions immediately lead us into the exceptionally intricate plot of a play in which so much is made about this and that, and into the various meanings of the word "nothing" that the dramatist puts into his play.

First, it seems as if the main plot, on the customarily aristocratic level, is divided in two, centering on the love affairs of Claudio and Hero, Benedick and Beatrice. The latter affair seems to be the simpler one, corresponding to the love between Lucentio and Bianca in *The Taming of the Shrew*, and the latter the more complicated, like that between Petruchio and Katharina. But it isn't so simple as that. For the former comes to a climax, as we might expect, in a wedding ceremony, but then the bridegroom Claudio, instead of replying to the priest's formal question, "Will you?" with the equally formal "Yes!" shocks everyone with an unexpected "No!" And so, it seems, comedy is suddenly plunged into tragedy.

As for the latter plot, involving Claudio's friend Benedick and Hero's cousin Beatrice, its complication arises from the fact that neither is in love with the other, but they are only sparring partners in witty repartee—the one recalling Romeo's humorous friend Mercutio, and the other Orlando's witty lover Rosalind. Complication further arises from the fact that Claudio conspires with his patron Don Pedro, Prince of Arragon, to devise a trap for the unwilling pair, so as to make them fall in love with each other. Much of the play is thus devoted to plotting and spying on these comic characters, so as to bring them together without their realizing it. At the same time, Don Pedro's bastard brother Don John is plotting against his brother and Claudio, so as to bring the latter's marriage down in ruins. It is Don John's plan to show them one of his henchmen, with the aid of a servant, climbing into Hero's window on the eve of the wedding. Claudio, who has seen it taking place, decides to disrupt the wedding ceremony the next morning. Then it is Beatrice's simple command to Benedick, if he is indeed her true lover, to "kill Claudio!" that brings the two plots to a seemingly tragic catastrophe.

This is, of course, not a tragedy but a comedy, and so out of such a catastrophe there has to be a happy *dénouement*. All is now in the hands partly of a wise friar (the priest who was officiating at the wedding ceremony, Friar Francis) and partly of a fool (the village constable, Dogberry, with his partner, or "headborough," Verges). The former devises a plan—reminiscent of that devised with less success by Friar Laurence for Juliet—for Hero to put on a show of death, with the advice, "Come, lady, die to live!" (iv.1). The village constable, without meaning to do so, somehow manages to arrest the culprit, Don John's henchman Borachio. On confessing his part in the plot, Borachio says to his judges, "What your wisdoms could not discover, these shallow fools have brought to light" (v.1). Such is the typical theme that Shakespeare delights to illustrate in his fools, derived partly from Psalm viii: "Out of the mouths of babes and sucklings thou hast perfected praise," and partly from St. Paul's first letter to the Corinthians: "God hath chosen the foolish things of the world to confound the wise" (i.27).

Thus, unlike *Romeo and Juliet,* where the dramatist may plead—like the poet in *Troilus and Criseyde*—that he has to keep to the story as he has received it from his source, *Much Ado About Nothing* has a happy ending. Here the "much ado" caused by Claudio at the wedding is countered by the "much ado" of the judges to extract a sensible statement from the village constable and his partner. There is also the "much ado" resorted to by Don Pedro and Claudio to convince first Benedick, then Beatrice, that they are in love with each other. As for the "nothing," its echo may be heard in the "No!" of Claudio at the wedding, and in his expostulation, echoing the words of Christ on the cross: "What men daily do, not knowing what they do!" It may also be heard in the friar's advice—"Come, lady, die to live!"—that leads to a strange exchange of "nothings" between Benedick and Beatrice, until she turns on him with the abrupt command, "Kill Claudio!" (iv.1).

Needless to say, Benedick doesn't kill Claudio, but eventually they are reconciled when Claudio learns of Hero's death and becomes convinced of her innocence. Then he is brought from "nothing" in his loss of Hero to all things by means of repentance, according to the saying later put by Shakespeare into the mouth of Timon of Athens, "Nothing brings me all things" (v.1). Then on reflection we realize how the whole play has been "much ado about nothing," not only (as noted above) in the sense of that Aristotelian nothing of which nothing will come (as Lear warns Cordelia), but also the nothing to which Hero is reduced in her seeming death so that she may thereby come to a seeming resurrection. Nor is it only that, but (according to a common Elizabethan pronunciation of the word) "nothing" may also have the meaning of "noting," or spying, with which this play is filled, as if in anticipation of *Hamlet*, while reflecting the underground world of Elizabethan Catholicism. There is also the "noting," or the singing of musical notes, which is oddly emphasized in the one scene that features the otherwise unnecessary singer named Balthazar. When invited by Don Pedro to sing, he makes the mock protest, "Note this before my notes, / There's not a note of mine that's worth the noting," to which Don Pedro responds in like vein, "Notes, notes, forsooth, and nothing!" (ii.3). Faced with such a superfluous scene, we wonder why the dramatist included it in his play—only to face the probable answer, "Why, it is just much ado about nothing!" (or more practically, just to provide a superfluous player with a part).

Finally, we may return to the parallel noted above between this play and *Romeo and Juliet*. One point that is noticeable in Shakespeare's choice of stories to be made into plays is his desire to keep a just balance, or to make up for past deficiencies—a desire that is not unrelated to the basic theme of repentance running through them all. One particular deficiency in the preceding tragedy is the way he has allowed the genius of comedy, in the person of Mercutio, to be killed for the sake of the tragedy—besides having left him without a lady (which was just as well in view of his tragic ending). This deficiency, however, he now remedies in *Much Ado About Nothing*, where the star performers are not Claudio and Hero but Benedick and Beatrice. Then in Benedick, the dramatist has provided us with a resurrection of Mercutio, and in Beatrice, he has provided Benedick with a suitable lady.

Another point worthy of note is the way Shakespeare arranges his plays, not in the conventional grouping of comedies, histories, and tragedies, or tetralogies or trilogies of history plays, or problem plays, or Roman plays, or final romances, but in an ongoing development of theme. In these two plays, therefore, the one a tragedy and the other a comedy, we come upon the presence of two friars, Laurence and Francis, as spiritual advisers and go-betweens for the lovers, and an anticipation of the Jacobean comedy of *Measure for Measure*, with yet a third friar, or rather a duke posing as Friar Lodowick and assisting the lovers in their problem of life and death. This trilogy is bound yet more impressively together by the names of the lovers—first Romeo and Juliet, then Claudio and Hero, and finally Claudio and Juliet—in a veritable "syllogism" of names.

■ *Twelfth Night, or What You Will*

The first question that naturally arises in our minds about the title of *Twelfth Night* is: To which night does it refer? In English Christian tradition the holy season of Christmas—hailed by Shakespeare in the opening scene of *Hamlet*, "So hallow'd and so gracious is the time"—is celebrated over a period of twelve days, culminating in the feast of the Epiphany on January 6, for the coming of the wise men to adore the divine Child at Bethlehem. Paradoxically, this feast of the wise men was also (like that of the Holy Innocents on December 28) celebrated as a feast of fools, when fools were allowed extra liberty and even dominion. So if a deeper significance is to be sought in the simplicity of this title, as a play for "twelfth night," it may be interpreted in terms of the contrast between the many fools, of whom it is said (in Eccl i.15), "Infinite is the multitude of fools," and the few wise men. This significance is underlined by the words of the Fool, in his statement (echoing Ecclesiastes), "Foolery, sir, does walk about the orb like the sun, it shines everywhere" (iii.1). Except that for Shakespeare, folly is rather to be found in the seemingly wise of this world, while true wisdom is to be found in fools and heroines.

The particular form taken by folly in this play is the madness engendered by the so-called humor of melancholy (or black choler), which affects all the major characters with two notable exceptions. The setting for the stage is the land of Illyria, presumably the capital city, where two houses (families) are located in opposite corners. One is the house of the noble duke Orsino, and the other, the house of the countess Olivia, with whom the duke professes to have fallen in love. On the one hand, the duke gives vent to the melancholy of love in his opening speech, "If music be the food of love, play on, / Give me excess of it that, surfeiting, / The appetite may sicken and so die!" His is not so much true love as fancy, or self-love, with regard more to himself and his mood of love than to its object in Olivia—to whom he makes his love known not so much in person as by means of ambassadors of love. It is the Fool who truly reads his character with the remark, "Now the melancholy god protect thee, and the tailor make thy doublet of changeable taffeta, for thy mind is a very opal" (ii.4).

On the other hand, the countess Olivia is prey to a somewhat different species of melancholy in that she has long been in mourning over "a brother's dead love," such that "like a cloistress" she will go about veiled "and water once a day her chamber round / With eye-offending brine" (i.1). At least, that is her excuse for not receiving Orsino's troublesome embassies of love. But once she comes upon a young and attractive ambassador like Viola, in male disguise as Cesario, she forgets all about her brother and promptly falls in love with her visitor. Thus from the outset we have that typical "love triangle," which is for Shakespeare the very prescription for comedy. Also in the house of Olivia, though not in that of Orsino, we come upon a contrast between two levels and two plots: the aristocratic level, including Olivia herself and Viola on her occasional visits, and the plebeian level of low life, including Olivia's boisterous uncle Sir Toby Belch with his worthless friend Sir Andrew Aguecheek, as well as her servants, the puritanical steward Malvolio and her witty handmaid Maria. There is also a contrast, as usual in the comedies, between the opposite media of verse (for the main plot) and prose (for the subplot). However, here, pride of place is accorded to the subplot, and so to the medium of prose, since it is chiefly for "the humours of Malvolio" that the play has from the beginning come to be appreciated by audiences.

Turning now to Viola, as the true heroine of the play, she has been wrecked on the coast of Illyria together with her twin brother Sebastian, but they have been rescued separately in such a way that each is convinced the other has been drowned—as it were, in a replay of *The Comedy of Errors*. Learning about the country and its noble duke, Viola proposes to go by herself, in male disguise, to the ducal court, and that is how she comes to be employed by the duke as his ambassador of love to Olivia. So it is, in earnestly pleading with the countess on behalf of the duke, she finds the countess has fallen in love with her, whereas she has already fallen in love with the duke. At the same time, because of her disguise and her embassy, she can observe the goings-on in either house with a certain impartiality, objectivity, and even humor—the very qualifications for that wisdom with which Shakespeare endows her, corresponding to the mediaeval ideal of the Virgin Mary as "Seat of Wisdom." Like the other heroines, moreover, she can appreciate the hidden wisdom of the Fool, on whom she makes the perceptive comment: "This fellow's wise enough to play the fool" (iii.1). The Fool, whose name is appropriately Feste for the Feast of Fools, also moves at ease between either house, while remaining aloof from them as he both laughs at their melancholy and is laughed at by them for his seeming folly.

Of the two it is the main plot that remains on the superficial level of love affairs, among those who have nothing else with which to occupy their empty minds. Rather, the main interest of the play attaches to the subplot, centering on the morose character of Olivia's steward Malvolio. His salient form of "humour" is a surliness of self-regard, as Olivia tells him to his face, "O, you are sick of self-love, Malvolio, and taste with a distempered appetite!" (i.5). From the viewpoint of his fellow servants, he is "a kind of Puritan," not so much in the religious sense as in the applied sense of "a time pleaser" (as Maria says of him, ii.3). He is all too ready to reprove others for their offenses, particularly Sir Toby for keeping late hours singing and drinking with his friend Sir Andrew. But Sir Toby is ready with his famous reply, "Dost thou think, because thou art virtuous, there shall be no more cakes and ale?" (ii.3). Malvolio is thus the perfect object for their communal teasing or leg-pulling, which now forms the main part of this delightful subplot— at the Puritans' expense. (It is often emphasized on behalf of the Puritans that Maria qualifies her remark with the disclaimer, "The devil a Puritan that he is, or anything constantly but a time-pleaser!" But in fact, such was the reputation of the Puritans in the Elizabethan age.)

The leg-pulling is centered on a pretended love letter supposedly written by Olivia to Malvolio, but really by Maria in Olivia's hand, and the letter is dropped by the conspirators— who in this respect seem to come straight out of *Much Ado*

About Nothing—on the garden path in the way of Malvolio. As he reads it to himself (in their hearing), he finds himself advised to wear "yellow stockings" and to be "cross-gartered" in a fashion that Maria knows to be abhorrent to Olivia, as well as to smile in his lady's presence. And so he does, the next time he comes before the countess, filling her with amazement—and the others with amusement. Olivia therefore puts him in charge of her uncle, who has the steward placed in a dark room, as a lunatic. While there, the Fool visits him in the garb of a minister come to visit the sick man in prison in the very climax of this comedy. Ironically, while Malvolio is said to be "a kind of Puritan," it is the Fool who assumes the air of a Puritan minister. Then, it may be added, even Malvolio's tormentors, Sir Toby and Maria, mouth Lutheran doctrine: Sir Toby, when he says of Viola on her first visit to Olivia, "Let him be the devil [of Lechery] and he will, I care not. Give me faith, say I!" (i.5), and Maria, when she brings news of the success of their trick on Malvolio, "There is no Christian that means to be saved by believing rightly, can ever believe such impossible passages of grossness" (as those expressed in the love letter and put into practice by the steward) (iii.2). In each case, their words imply belief in Luther's doctrine of salvation by faith alone.

Now the complications of the plot become even more complicated, and the confusions more confounded, with the unexpected arrival of Sebastian, who appears as the spit image of his sister Viola, especially as she is now wearing male attire. A climax comes when Olivia proposes to him and he gladly accepts her love, with the astonished reaction—recalling that of Bottom concerning Titania—"This is the air, that the glorious sun!" She must be quite mad, he thinks, and yet she rules her house with prudence. His feeling is rather one of wonder, recalling that of the Athenian lovers on waking from their midsummer night's dream (iv.1). It is also the feeling that the dramatist is concerned to elicit in the spectators of all his comedies. Then there comes a further climax when the twins are at last shown together, and it is the duke's turn to express his feeling of wonder: "One face, one voice, one habit, and two persons, / A natural perspective, that is and is not!" (v.1). And so, while Olivia has her Sebastian, if as a result of misunderstanding, Viola has her Orsino, or in the more general terms employed by Puck in *A Midsummer Night's Dream*, "Jack shall have Jill, / Nought shall go ill" (iii.2).

Moreover, if we accept the reconstruction of *The First Night of Twelfth Night* by Leslie Hotson (1954), the play would have been first presented as a court performance at Whitehall for Queen Elizabeth and her noble Italian guest, Don Virginio Orsino, Duke of Bracciano, on January 6, 1601. Then if in terms of the play Orsino is Duke of Illyria, who is the countess Olivia but Queen Elizabeth herself, still unmarried as though in prolonged mourning for her dead brother, Edward VI? From a religious viewpoint, however, here is a Catholic duke, whose duchy happens to be within the Papal States, venturing (without permission) on a state visit to the Protestant queen of England, and here is a Catholic dramatist entertaining them with what might be interpreted as an ecumenical gesture far in advance of his time. Unlike his previous *As You Like It*, there is in this play little of Papist reference, save insofar as Shakespeare, with his hidden Catholicism, may have been playing on that dislike of Puritans which Elizabethan Catholics shared with Elizabeth herself.

But when we attend to the dating of the play, January 6, 1601, we may notice that it was presented at court a bare month before the ill-fated Essex rebellion, in which Shakespeare himself was involved with his company. On the eve of that rebellion, on February 6, certain followers of Essex persuaded the Chamberlain's Men to present a revival of the old play of *Richard II*, with the scene of the king's deposition. Then in the aftermath of the fiasco, the players became suspect along with the earls of Essex and Southampton of the capital crime of treason. Even the queen is said to have recognized herself in the person of Richard, angrily muttering to one of her courtiers, "I am Richard II, know ye not that?" Fortunately, the players were let off on the plea of ignorance. In any case, the queen would have been reluctant to charge her favorite players and their dramatist with such a crime, but she was still angry at them. And so it would have been wise for them to lie low for a time and to stay away from the city, perhaps even venturing as far north as Edinburgh.

chapter 9
Hamlet

Hamlet

IT IS NOT uncommon for scholars to express surprise at
the sudden change from such a happy comedy as *Twelfth
Night* to such a problem tragedy as *Hamlet*. This is because
they are all too willing to remain on the level of outward
appearances, without searching the depths of Shakespeare's
mind for the inner causes of the melancholy that strangely
links the characters of Malvolio (or malcontent) and Hamlet. Already in *Twelfth Night*, before the outbreak of the
Essex rebellion, we have noticed the widespread melancholy
as well in Orsino and Olivia as in Malvolio, and so that play
can hardly be described as "the happiest of Shakespeare's
happy comedies," though it may be called the funniest.
Also, in the outcome, when the cruel plot against Malvolio
has been exposed, much to the discomfiture of the poor victim, we have his last recorded words, "I'll be reveng'd on the
whole pack of you!" (v.1). Thus at the end of the play we are
left with an aftertaste of revenge, as if to prepare our minds
for another revenge that is soon to follow.

Then, too, when we cast our minds back on the other
"happy comedies" (as named by J. Dover Wilson in 1962),
we may recognize how the theme of jealousy is taken up from

Claudio's reaction to Hero in *Much Ado About Nothing* and reenacted in tragic mode in *Othello*. We may also recognize how the themes of exile and family conflict are taken up from *As You Like It*, as well as *Richard II*, and given a cosmic and tragic dimension in *King Lear*. Yet again, the ending of *Twelfth Night*, with the strangely melancholic song of Feste—on finding himself left alone (like Antonio at the end of *The Merchant of Venice*) in solitary bachelorhood, while others have all found lovers for themselves—"When that I was and a little tiny boy, / With hey, ho, the wind and the rain," is taken up by his tragic counterpart the Fool in *King Lear*, "He that has a little tiny wit, / With hey, ho, the wind and the rain" (iii.2).

As for the play of *Hamlet*, which surely comes after *Twelfth Night* and probably after the death of Shakespeare's father, John, in the autumn of 1601, it is more accurately to be categorized as a problem play than as either a tragedy or a revenge play. Needless to say, there are many tragedies lumped together in the closing scene of the play, but, as Horatio says of them, they are but "accidental judgments, casual slaughters" and "purposes mistook / Fall'n on the inventors' heads" (v.2), serving but to deepen the sense of doubt rather than of tragedy. Even Hamlet's revenges against his principal enemies, Claudius and Polonius, not to mention his opponent in the last duel, Laertes, and the pair of spies, Rosencrantz and Guildenstern, take place by accident, with little forethought at least on his part. From the outset this problematic nature of the play is stated by Marcellus in his doubtful words, "Something is rotten in the state of Denmark" (i.4), but it has already been personified in the form of "the majesty of buried Denmark," the ghost of Hamlet's father (i.1). The very mention of the ghost's appearance reported by Horatio to Hamlet in the second scene prompts the latter to respond with a series of questions. A similar response is elicited from him on his actual confrontation with the ghost in the fourth scene: "Say, why is this? Wherefore? What should we do?" Such is the extent to which the young hero feels his disposition shaken "with thoughts beyond the reaches" of his soul (i.4). True, the ghost reappears only once more, in the closet scene between Hamlet and his mother (iii.4), but, like the ghost of Julius Caesar once he has been assassinated in Act III of his play, that of Hamlet's father remains a continued, if unseen, presence from first to last—as it were, hovering over the whole play, like a vast mushroom cloud of devastation.

This problematic nature of *Hamlet* is further underlined by a new, unusual departure of the dramatist in his characterization of heroines—if we may count Hamlet's mother Gertrude and his presumed lover Ophelia as heroines. Up to this play Shakespeare has invariably presented us with ideal heroines—even when they only become ideal in the course of the play, like Katharina in *The Taming of the Shrew*—characterizing them in terms of divine grace, as it were, in honor of the Virgin Mary. Now, however, as though revealing how deeply the problems of life have sunk into his very soul, Hamlet exclaims, with reference to his mother, "Frailty, thy name is woman!" (i.2). That exclamation he also extends to his seeming lover Ophelia, both in the "nunnery" scene (iii.1) and in the subsequent scene of the play-within-the-play when he is abominably rude to her, hinting that she is little better than a harlot. Evidently he has no feeling for her, or for others—with the possible exception of his friend Horatio—or even for himself, as he roughly tells Ophelia, "We are arrant knaves all, believe none of us!" (iii.1). Indeed, we are disposed to take him at his word and to regard him, for all his princely qualities, as an arrant knave! "O, what a

noble mind is here o'erthrown!" laments poor Ophelia—and
we are tempted to transfer her opinion of Hamlet to Shakespeare himself, as revealed in this play. Can this really, we
wonder, be "the gentle Shakespeare" of legend?

As a result of the ghost's appearance we notice not one
but two problems confronting Hamlet. First, there is his
strange distemper as noticed by all around him, leading
them to wonder (as we have been wondering about his creator) what on earth has happened to him. Is this, we ask, the
outcome of his decision, which he has confided to his
friends, "To put an antic disposition on" (i.5)? Or is it that,
having seen the ghost, he has himself become deranged, as
he goes on to admit to his schoolmates who have been sent
to spy on him, "I am but mad north-north-west" (ii.2)? He
is indeed mad—more than he realizes—and his pretense of
madness is but a disguise for the reality. But why is he mad?
That is the question. It is to ascertain the answer that
Claudius sets spies on Hamlet, then arranges with Polonius
their own little play-within-the-play in the "nunnery scene"
between Hamlet and Ophelia. Then we wonder if Hamlet is
aware of their spying on him in this scene, in a situation of
mutual espionage. In that case, he is perhaps purposely mis-
leading them, first with his soliloquy, "To be, or not to
be"—which has nothing to do with his real situation, but
more to do with his reading of the Book of Job—and then
with his rough treatment of Ophelia, whom he regards as
their willing decoy (iii.1).

Then there is the further problem in Hamlet's mind: How
far can he trust the bare word of a ghost, who may after all be
the devil masquerading as a ghost and abusing him to damn
him (ii.2)? He therefore considers it incumbent on himself to
find out if what the ghost has told him about Claudius is
true or not. So when a group of players arrives on a visit to

the castle, he welcomes them both as players and as a heaven-sent opportunity for discovering the truth, exclaiming, "The play's the thing / Wherein I'll catch the conscience of the king" (ii.2). Now not only is Hamlet being spied upon by his enemies, but he is also spying on them with counterintelligence, and not just on their outer actions but on their inner thoughts or "conscience." In this keyword we may also discern two meanings. On their side, Claudius and Polonius are spying on the intellectual "consciousness" of Hamlet to find out how much he knows of what Ulysses in the next play of *Troilus and Cressida* calls the "mystery in the soul of state" (iii.3), while on his side, Hamlet is more interested in the moral "conscience" of Claudius, to find out if he is really guilty of the murder of his royal father.

All this mutual espionage leads up to the climactic events of Act III, beginning with the two plays-within-the-play. The first, staged by Claudius and Polonius using Ophelia as a decoy for Hamlet, turns out to be inconclusive from the viewpoint of Claudius, partly because Hamlet is no doubt aware of being spied upon. The second, staged by Hamlet on them, convinces him of Claudius's guilt, when the king runs from the hall calling for light. Hamlet's play is, in fact, more successful than he realizes, as he has indeed caught the troubled conscience of the king, so as to transform him from villain even to victim. Such is the point of Claudius's soliloquy, "O, my offence is rank, it smells to heaven!" (iii.3)—which Hamlet no more heeds than Claudius or Polonius heeded his own soliloquy. For now Claudius is turning to repentance, while Hamlet, passing behind him at prayer, holds his hand from revenge only at the thought that in this way he would merely be sending Claudius's soul to heaven instead of hell. Thus it is that while Claudius is on his way upward to good as victim, Hamlet is on his way down to evil as villain!

In fact, however, Claudius fails to repent. For he is unwilling to give up "those effects for which I did the murder, / My crown, mine own ambition, and my queen" (iii.3). Then Hamlet goes on to confront his mother in her closet with what she has done. At first she betrays no sign of guilt, but when her son forces her to look into her very soul, she confesses that there "I see such black and grained spots / As will not leave their tinct" (iii.4). So he brings her to an insight into her own conscience and to a genuine repentance, which is proved even to the end, when it seems she dies to save her son from being poisoned by the cup prepared for him. Meanwhile, in Hamlet himself—for all his self-righteousness, in professing to serve the heavens as "their scourge and minister," and for all his appeal to "conscience" as self-justification both in killing Claudius and in sending Rosencrantz and Guildenstern to their certain deaths in England (v.2)—we can find little sign of a real conscience. For all his aptitude to reflect on human life and death, there is no interiority about him. All is mere posing, the self-dramatizing of an immature student! And his admirers, from Goethe to Bloom, are merely deceiving themselves!

It is in Act III, with its four successive and impressive scenes, that the plotting of these "mighty opposites" (v.2) comes to an undignified close. Now Hamlet is justly banished to England, owing to his "accidental" murder of the old Polonius, when, he avers, "I took thee for thy better" (iii.4), though he knew perfectly well what he was doing. Now his lover Ophelia goes mad, deprived at once of her father by death and her lover by banishment. In her confused imagination she even mixes up their identities, as if she has really been more in love with her father than with Hamlet, just as we may suspect Hamlet of having been more in love with his mother than with Ophelia. Consequently, the action of Act IV turns largely on this madness of poor Ophelia, and that serves as an incentive for her returned brother Laertes to seek the death of Hamlet as the one responsible for the deaths of father and, later, sister.

Then the situation changes, in a sudden reversal worthy of Agatha Christie, as Hamlet succeeds in escaping from the ship bearing him and his schoolmates (as his guards) to England, so that he reaches Denmark in time to witness the funeral of Ophelia with its "maimed rites," as if she has committed suicide (v.1). This is such a famous scene, showing Hamlet at his most morbid, reflecting in the graveyard on the theme of death and decay, holding up the skull of his old jester Yorick and holding forth on the commonplace student theme of *"Ubi sunt qui ante nos in mundo fuere?"*— Where are they who were before us in this world? These words are all too often quoted as evidence of his philosophic temperament, as a humanist of the Renaissance, but all his humanism is merely derived secondhand from the University of Wittenberg (Luther's university), which has also provided Hamlet with his pessimistic ideas about fallen man and this sinful world. If Malvolio was "a kind of Puritan," may we not say the same of Hamlet, self-righteous in himself and critical of others, including the clowns who are even now engaged in digging Ophelia's grave and singing (much to Hamlet's scandal) at their task.

Still, we may ask, is Hamlet altogether a Puritan like Falstaff and Sir Toby, Maria and Malvolio, or even Polonius and his family? No, I dare answer. He is too complex a character to be a simple Puritan. He may have received a Puritan, or at least a Lutheran, formation at Wittenberg, producing in him an excessive awareness of sin, as well as a tendency to criticize others. But on his return to Denmark we find him sympathizing, in accordance with his natural instinct, rather with the old order, represented by the ghost of his father, than with the new order, represented by Claudius and Gertrude, with the necessary help of Polonius. For so Claudius has assured Laertes, "The head is not more native to the heart, / The hand more instrumental to the mouth, / Than is the throne of Denmark to thy father" (i.2). Put in contemporary Elizabethan terms, this would make Hamlet more a Papist than a Puritan—terms that are positively demanded of a play that places early mediaeval Denmark so squarely in early modern England.

In that case, we may ask, who is Gertrude but Queen Elizabeth? And who is Claudius but her lover, though never spouse, Robert Dudley, Earl of Leicester? And who is Polonius but Sir William Cecil, Lord Burghley, Elizabeth's chief minister through forty years of her long reign (from 1558 till his death in 1598) and chief architect of the so-called religious settlement of Queen Elizabeth? Apart from the similarity of the name of Polonius to that of Burghley (allowing for a Welsh pronunciation, with "p" for "b," of the Latinized name), we may note the passion of Polonius, as of Burghley, to "find / Where truth is hid, though it were hid indeed / Within the centre" (ii.2)—with regard not only to Hamlet, but even to his own son Laertes during his studies in Paris. We may also note the long-winded advice Polonius bestows on that son before his going to Paris, echoing that given by Lord Burghley to his son. Then we may note the subservient, deferential manner observed by Polonius to the king and queen, and his general fussiness in going about affairs, which offers Hamlet a perfect target for ridicule—obscuring for many critics the fact that behind all his doddering there is a sinister politician at work, if in dotage.

It is against all this that Hamlet reacts so violently, even to the extent of killing Polonius with the words, "Thou wretched, rash, intruding fool, farewell!" (iii.4). This is perhaps already at the back of his mind when, in the hearing of Polonius and Claudius, he comes out with his famous soliloquy, "To be, or not to be" (iii.1). In itself, as I have suggested, the soliloquy is abstract, impersonal, objective, hardly touching on the events in the play, and so different from Hamlet's opening soliloquy, "O, that this too, too solid flesh would melt!" (i.2). In it the hero isn't speaking about himself at all, but merely using verbs in the infinitive, or if he mentions human beings it is only in the plural "we" or the indefinite "he." Only when he comes to his last sentence and notices Ophelia at prayer, he tenderly petitions her, "Nymph, in thy orisons / Be all my sins remember'd" (iii.1).

All the same, it is to be noted that the question Hamlet asks, if in infinitive terms, isn't just the seemingly metaphysical "to be, or not to be" (as if he were some existentialist student at the Sorbonne following the lectures of Sartre). It is more precisely, as he goes on to define it, "to suffer the slings and arrows of outrageous fortune" (which is how he conceives "to be") or "to take arms against a sea of troubles, / And by opposing end them" (which is how he conceives "not to be"). Then to whom, we may ask, in the contemporary situation of Shakespeare's England would this dilemma be more applicable than to the poor, persecuted Catholics, suffering as they were under increasingly stepped-up pressure from Elizabeth and Leicester and especially the spymaster (and rack-master) Lord Burghley? For the Catholics, the almost daily dilemma was that between continuing to endure the unendurable, as their pastors, the Jesuits and seminary priests, were ever urging them to do, and having resort to some such desperate measure as killing the queen or at least supporting the rebellion of the noble Earl of Essex against the queen and her advisers. Among those supporters was, we know, Shakespeare's patron, the Earl of Southampton, and his cousin (on his mother's side) Robert Catesby, as well as other Catholics who looked to Essex (though himself a favorer of Protestantism) for a measure of toleration.

Thus it is that in Hamlet's mind we have a confused mixture of Protestant doctrine and Catholic allegiance. So, too, in the ghost we find something of the old Catholic belief in purgatory, as he professes to come from a "prison-house" in which he is "confin'd to fast in fires, / Till the foul crimes done in my days of nature / Are burnt and purg'd away" (i.5). And yet we are left in doubt whether or not "he may be the devil," who abuses Hamlet to damn him, according to the Protestant explanation of ghosts. Or he may even be a pagan ghost, rising from the old plays of the Roman Seneca, with his characteristic appeal for revenge. All this Shakespeare seems to leave in a state of calculated confusion, as it were, reflecting the mentality of not a few Englishmen of the time, notably the poet John Donne, who came from an even more devoutly Catholic background than Shakespeare but went on to apostatize from his "old faith."

As for the outcome, there seems to be some kind of spiritual renewal or regeneration in the soul of Hamlet on his providential return from England. At least, in recalling the way he managed to escape from his ship, with the assistance of pirates whom he calls "thieves of mercy" (iv.6), he draws the pious conclusion, "And that should teach us / There's a divinity that shapes our ends, / Rough-hew them how we will" (v.2). Then, finding his father's seal in his possession, which he needed for resealing the document his guards were bringing with them to England for his immediate death, he adds, "Why, even in that was heaven ordinant!" Third, with more explicit reference to the words of Christ, he declares, "There's a special providence in the fall of a sparrow. . . .

The readiness is all" (cf. Matt x.29, xxiv.44). These words, coming as they do one upon another in the same scene, seem to indicate a spiritual rebirth in Hamlet. Yet in spite of them all, Hamlet almost immediately goes on to enact a bloody revenge, involving not only Laertes and Claudius, but also Gertrude and himself, not to mention the reported deaths of poor Rosencrantz and Guildenstern, as well as the earlier deaths of Polonius and Ophelia. It is indeed a "bloody period"! (*Othello* v.2).

No wonder spectators leave the theatre at the end of the play in a depressed state of mind. Here one feels nothing of the *catharsis*, or purification of emotion, that Aristotle expects of a tragedy and that Shakespeare provides us with at the end of *King Lear*. To the very end we are left with the problem of Hamlet unsolved. And that is exactly what prompted T. S. Eliot to make his famous remark about *Hamlet* falling short of the ideal of dramatic art, though it might be added, in the words of Alexander Pope, that in this play the dramatist has snatched "a grace beyond the reach of art."

Troilus and Cressida

Shakespeare seems to have regarded it as a privilege of his dramatic genius to nod off, like Homer, after having produced a great drama like *Hamlet*. It is as if after a climax there has to be an anticlimax, and after the storm of dramatic tension there has to come the peace of relaxation. Thus it is that the great dramatist follows up his masterpiece of *Hamlet*, which is undeniably one of the masterpieces of world literature, with such a crabbed problem play as *Troilus and Cressida*. Unlike *Timon of Athens*, which may be interpreted as serving a similar function of anticlimax to either *King Lear* or *Macbeth*, this play doesn't even have the excuse of being unfinished. It was finished but was apparently never acted in the dramatist's own lifetime, nor even till the twentieth century—except for a brief period at the time of the Restoration, when it was rewritten by John Dryden in 1679. The language is much too heavy, and heavily satirical, as though destined for a sophisticated audience of lawyers and legal students, but it was evidently too much even for them—to judge from the strange epistle attached to a reissue of the first quarto of 1609, describing this as "a new play, never staled with the stage, never clapper-clawed with the palms of the vulgar."

In that epistle the play is called a comedy, but in the First Folio it is included among the tragedies. In fact, however, it is neither the one nor the other but a problem play, like *Hamlet*, leaving the spectator at the end with a feeling of disappointment, if not disillusionment. In common with all Shakespeare's plays, especially those of his maturity, *Troilus and Cressida* has many good things in it, some memorable speeches and sentences, but they all seem to pull in different directions and fail to come together in any real dramatic unity. As a whole, the play is set in the epic background of the Siege of Troy, with a contrast between the aristocratic Trojan princes, centered on their hero Hector, and the plebeian Greeks, among whom democracy has degenerated into an individualistic chaos represented not so much by their generals, Agamemnon and Achilles, as by the foul-mouthed common soldier Thersites. In the foreground we are shown the doubtful love affair between the young, impulsive Trojan prince Troilus and the alluring, artful Cressida. Here, like Antony lamenting the downfall of Julius Caesar, one feels like lamenting the dramatist's own downfall in this play: "O, what a fall was there, my countrymen!" (*Julius Caesar* iii.2).

Unlike the innocent, youthful love of Romeo and Juliet, the love or lust portrayed in *Troilus and Cressida* is frankly sensual, swayed more by sexual appetite than human reason. They are, moreover, assisted not by any friar, such as Friar Laurence or Friar Francis, but by Cressida's bawdy uncle Pandarus, whose delight is (as his name implies) to pander to their mutual appetite. His idea of love, as introduced by his song, "Love, love, nothing but love, still more!" (iii.1), is nothing but lust. Such, too, is the feeling that possesses the heart of Troilus, as he exclaims, "I am giddy, expectation whirls me round. / The imaginary relish is so sweet / That it enchants my sense" (iii.2). And then, "Even such a passion doth embrace my bosom, / My heart beats thicker than a fev'rous pulse." On her side, the fickle Cressida admits, "I have a kind of self resides with you, / But an unkind self, that itself will leave, / To be another's fool."

Such a love cannot but, in Macbeth's words, be "cabin'd, cribb'd, confin'd" (iii.4) within the limits of place and time. So once Cressida goes over to the Greek camp, according to a treaty of peace between the warring armies, she is observed by the perspicacious Ulysses, "Fie, fie upon her! / There's language in her eye, her cheek, her lip, / Nay, her foot speaks!" (iv.5). She is a natural flirt, delighting in the attention of men, and it is not long before she accepts the smooth words and proposals of the Greek Diomede. Subsequently, she is actually witnessed by Troilus as "Diomed's Cressida," leading him to lament, "This is, and is not, Cressid," with the disillusioned conclusion, "The bonds of heaven are slipp'd, dissolv'd, and loos'd!" (v.2). This is for him a tragedy of the heart, but he remains alive, while Hector dies, killed by a mere trick of Achilles, with nothing of the epic dignity of Homer's *Iliad.*

In all this we may detect as it were a sequel to *Hamlet,* in point of style though not of subject, and notably in the disillusioned attitude of the dramatist toward such women as

Cressida and Helen of Troy, as if developed out of Ophelia and Gertrude. Here we have nothing of the virginal, divine grace that envelops the earlier Elizabethan heroines or the later Jacobean heroines—though in such women we may sense something of Shakespeare's feeling about the aging queen Elizabeth, as subsequently portrayed in the cunning art of Cleopatra or in the "shallow, changing woman" already presented in an earlier Elizabeth, widow to Edward IV (*Richard III*, iv.4).

It is in this political context, as the old queen was drawing to her earthly end, that we may understand two notable speeches put into the mouth of the wily Greek politician Ulysses. First, we have his speech on "degree," beginning, "The heavens themselves, the planets, and this centre [the earth] / Observe degree, priority and place, / . . . in all line of order" (i.3). The words are evidently based on a passage in the opening of the homily "Of Obedience," and its idea is repeated more than once in Shakespeare's plays, including the part commonly assigned to him in the collaborative play *Sir Thomas More* (which never won the approval of the censor). It seems to express a basic idea in Shakespeare's plays as well as in what E. M. W. Tillyard calls "the Elizabethan world picture" (see Tillyard's 1943 book of the same name). Yet it has to be remembered (a) that the source states the typical party line of the Church of England, with which the dramatist, as a Catholic, could hardly have been in agreement; (b) that the person to whom the words are assigned is a wily politician, and the dramatist is evidently of Sir Andrew's opinion in *Twelfth Night*, that "I had as lief be a Brownist [an extreme Puritan] as a politician" (iii.2); and (c) that the date commonly accepted for the play, 1601–2, is all but contemporaneous with *Hamlet* and composed in the aftermath of the Essex rebellion, in which Shakespeare and his company were deeply involved. In such circumstances one is tempted to identify the politician Ulysses with the chief enemy of Essex and the main object of his rebellion, Sir Robert Cecil, who had by now made himself no less indispensable to the old queen than his father, Sir William Cecil, Lord Burghley.

This identification becomes even more probable when we turn to the second speech of Ulysses mentioned above: "There is a mystery—with whom relation / Durst never meddle—in the soul of state, / Which hath an operation more divine / Than breath or pen can give expressure to" (iii.3). This is no mere commonplace, like the foregoing speech on "degree," but a deeply sinister, satirical comment on the secrecy of Tudor politics, in which few were more deeply involved than the two Cecils, father and son, and which is more accurately, if less ironically, to be described as "diabolic" than "divine." In this way we may see the characterization of Ulysses as looking forward to that of Iago in the first play of the new reign, *Othello*.

The End of the Elizabethan Age

From the beginning of his career on the London stage, we have noticed the strange ease with which Shakespeare, though a common player, seems to have mixed with the high and mighty of the realm—with Lord Strange, soon to become Earl of Derby on the death of his father the fourth earl; with the Earl of Southampton; with the Lord Chamberlain and Lord Hunsdon, father and son, close cousins to the queen; and possibly with the queen herself. Lord Strange would, of course, have been Shakespeare's first patron in the group of Strange's Men, perhaps from the dramatist's days in Lancashire, and it was no doubt of Lord Strange (whose personal name was Ferdinand) that Shakespeare was thinking in giving the name of Ferdinand to the king of Navarre in the early comedy of *Love's Labour's Lost.*

Second, the young Catholic Earl of Southampton, Henry Wriothesley, was certainly the nobleman to whom Shakespeare dedicated his two long poems, *Venus and Adonis* in 1593 and *The Rape of Lucrece* in 1594, and was probably the "young man" of the sonnets, which were evidently composed about the same time. Among the sonnets, most of them written in the same period as *Love's Labour's Lost* and *Romeo and Juliet,* and in the same lyrical vein, we find the poet affirming, on the one hand, that "our undivided loves are one" (xxxv) and lamenting, on the other, that as a player, he has made himself "a motley to the view" (cx) and consequently unworthy of his noble friend. It is also conjectured that some of the plays, notably *Love's Labour's Lost,* were presented in time of plague at Southampton's country mansion at Titchfield in Hampshire. Then, too, the names of Montague in *Romeo and Juliet* and Belmont in *The Merchant of Venice* echo those of Southampton's father-in-law Viscount Montague, of Cowdray in Sussex, and his cousin Thomas Pounde, of Belmont in Hampshire.

Third, passing over Lord Hunsdon, who was nominally patron to the Chamberlain's Men from their formation in 1594, but with whom the dramatist seems to have had no special connection, we may turn to the friend and ally of Southampton, the Earl of Essex. Among the followers of Essex, especially at the time of his rebellion in 1601, there were not a few Catholics, not only Southampton himself but also several of Shakespeare's relatives, including Robert Catesby, who went on to become the ringleader of the Gunpowder Plot conspirators in 1605. It was, as we have noted, on the very eve of the Essex rebellion that Shakespeare's company revived *Richard II,* thus implicating themselves in the rebellion and coming dangerously close to being charged with the crime of treason. Before then, in his Prologue to Act V of *Henry V* the dramatist went so far as to hail the earl as "the general of our gracious empress," who has led an English army to Ireland so as to bring "rebellion broached on his sword."

Finally, as for Queen Elizabeth herself, the dramatist seems to flatter her not only in the above words, as "our gracious empress," but also in *A Midsummer Night's Dream* as "a fair vestal [virgin] throned by the West" and as "the imperial votaress" (ii.1). Then there is the above-mentioned flattering identification of her in *Twelfth Night* with the countess Olivia, as the object of Orsino's love. There is also the tradition of how the queen became a fan of Falstaff, to such an extent that she desired the dramatist to compose a further play showing "Falstaff in love"—whose outcome is to be seen in *The Merry Wives of Windsor*. The suggestion has even been made, by George Bernard Shaw, that the notorious "dark lady" of the sonnets was none other than the queen. Yet another, even more far-fetched, suggestion is that the queen is to be credited with the real authorship of Shakespeare's plays! (To this theory it was objected that the author must have been a man, not a woman, but it was answered that the queen was in reality not a woman, but a man!)

On the other hand, a less favorable view of Elizabeth, in view of her indecision, which was often the despair of her ministers, may be discerned in Richard III's abusive remark on the earlier Elizabeth, widow to Edward IV, "Relenting fool, and shallow, changing woman!" (iv.4). She may also be identified with Gertrude, of whom Hamlet utters the general lament, "Frailty, thy name is woman!", and even with Ophelia, for her notorious use of cosmetics—even to the extent mentioned by Hamlet in the graveyard scene, "Now get you to my lady's chamber, and tell her, let her paint an inch thick, to this favour she must come!" (v.1). Then on the occasion of the queen's death in 1603 Shakespeare was taken to task by the contemporary poet Henry Chettle, in his *England's Mourning Garment* (1603), for his failure "to mourn her death that graced his desert." Only later, as noted above, in *Antony and Cleopatra* (dated 1607–8) is his memory of Queen Elizabeth seemingly incorporated into the character of Cleopatra, with Essex as Antony. The only real praise of Elizabeth is that put into the mouth of Archbishop Cranmer in the last scene of *Henry VIII*, which is generally attributed to the hand of Shakespeare's young collaborator John Fletcher.

And so we come with Shakespeare to the end of the long reign of Queen Elizabeth, invited to look, in the words of Achilles to Hector, "how the sun begins to set," and how "ugly night comes breathing at his heels" (v.8). Such is indeed the feeling he conveys in the ending of his two problem tragedies, but if the winter of his long discontent is coming to a close with the expiration of the old queen, can spring, he may well have asked himself (in anticipation of Shelley), be far behind? Yet it is with mixed feelings that he enters upon the new age of King James I, as a member of the newly formed King's Men, with darker tragedies than anything he has produced in the previous reign, while revealing a new kind of ideal heroine more intimately associated with divine grace than any of his past heroines.

Appendices

appendix 1
Classical Comments on Shakespeare

Ben Jonson (1572–1637)

From verses prefixed to the First Folio of 1623: "To the memory of my beloved, The Author Mr. William Shakespeare." "The wonder of our stage . . . / Thou art a monument without a tomb, / And art alive still, while thy book doth live . . . / And though thou hadst small Latin and less Greek . . . / He was not of an age but for all time . . . / Yet must I not give Nature all. Thy Art, / My gentle Shakespeare, must bear a part . . . / Sweet Swan of Avon!"

From *Timber, or Discoveries* (1640): "The players have often mentioned it as an honour to Shakespeare, that in his writing (whatsoever he penned) he never blotted out a line. My answer hath been, Would he had blotted out a thousand. . . . I loved the man, and do honour his memory on this side idolatry, as much as any. He was indeed honest, and of an open and free nature, and had an excellent fantasy, brave notions and gentle expressions, wherein he flowed with that facility that sometimes it was necessary that he should be stopped."

John Milton (1608–74)

From *L'Allegro* (c. 1631): "Or sweetest Shakespeare, Fancy's child, / Warble his native woodnotes wild."

From "An Epitaph on the admirable dramatic poet, W. Shakespeare," attached to the Second Folio of 1632: "What needs my Shakespeare for his honour'd bones, / The labour of an age, in piled stones / Or that his hallowed relics should be hid / Under a star-y-pointing pyramid? . . . / Thou in our wonder and astonishment / Hast built thyself a livelong monument . . . / And so sepulchred in such pomp dost lie / That kings for such a tomb would wish to die."

John Dryden (1631–1700)

From *Essay of Dramatic Poesy* (1668): "To begin then with Shakespeare, he was the man who of all modern and perhaps ancient poets had the largest and most comprehensive soul. All the images of Nature were still present to him and he drew them not laboriously but luckily. When he describes anything, you more than see it, you feel it too. Those who accuse him to have wanted learning give him the greater commendation. He was naturally learned. He needed not the spectacles of books to read Nature. He looked inwards and found her there."

From the Prologue to *Aureng-Zebe* (1675): "But spite of all his pride, a secret shame / Invades his breast at Shakespeare's sacred name."

Joseph Addison (1672–1719)

From *The Spectator* (July 1712): "Among the English Shakespeare has incomparably excelled all others. That noble extravagance of fancy, which he had in so great perfection, thoroughly qualified him to touch this weak superstitious part of his reader's imagination, and made him capable of succeeding, where he had nothing to support him besides the strength of his own genius. There is something so wild and yet so solemn in the speeches of his ghosts, fairies, witches and the like imaginary persons that we cannot forbear thinking them natural and must confess, if there are such beings in the world, it looks highly probable they should talk and act as he has represented them."

Alexander Pope (1688–1744)

From the preface to *The Works of Shakespeare* (1725): "If ever any author deserved the name of an original, it was Shakespeare. . . . The poetry of Shakespeare was inspiration indeed. He is not so much an imitator, as an instrument, of Nature. And 'tis not so just to say that he speaks from her, as that she speaks through him. The characters are so much Nature herself that 'tis a sort of injury to call them by so distant a name as copies of her. . . . Every single character in Shakespeare is as much an individual as those in life itself."

From the epistle "To Augustus" (1737): "Shakespeare (whom you and every play-house bill / Style the divine, the matchless, what you will) / For gain, not glory, wing'd his roving flight / And grew immortal in his own despite."

Samuel Johnson (1707–84)

From *Preface to Shakespeare* (1765): "Shakespeare is above all writers, at least above all modern writers, the poet of Nature, the poet that holds up to his readers a faithful mirror of manners and of life. His characters are not modified by the customs of particular places, unpractised by the rest of the world, by the peculiarities of studies or professions, which can operate but upon small numbers, or by the accidents of transient fashions or temporary opinions. They are the genuine progeny of common humanity, such as the world will always supply and observation will always find.

"Shakespeare's plays are not in the rigorous and critical sense either tragedies or comedies but compositions of a distinct kind, exhibiting the real state of sublunary Nature, which partakes of good and evil, joy and sorrow, mingled with endless variety and innumerable modes of combination and expressing the course of the world, in which the loss of one is the gain of another. . . . Shakespeare has united the powers of exciting laughter and sorrow not only in one mind but in one composition. Almost all his plays are divided between serious and ludicrous characters, and in the successive evolution of the design sometimes produce seriousness and sorrow, and sometimes levity and laughter.

"His first defect is that to which may be imputed most of the evil in books or in men. He sacrifices virtue to convenience, and is so much more careful to please than to instruct, that he seems to write without any moral purpose. From his writings indeed a system of moral duty may be selected, for he that thinks reasonably must think morally. But his precepts and axioms drop casually from him, he makes no just distribution of good or evil, nor is always careful to show in the virtuous a disapprobation of the wicked. He carries his persons indifferently through right and wrong, and at the close dismisses them without further care and leaves their examples to operate by chance.

"A quibble is to Shakespeare what luminous vapours are to the traveler. He follows it at all adventures. It is sure to lead him out of his way and sure to engulf him in the mire. It has some malignant power over his mind, and its fascinations are irresistible. Whatever be the dignity or profundity of his disquisition, whether he be enlarging knowledge or exalting affection, whether he be amusing attention with incidents or enchaining it in suspense, let but a quibble spring up before him, and he leaves his work unfinished. A quibble is the golden apple for which he will always turn aside from his career or stoop from his elevation. A quibble, poor and barren as it is, gave him such delight that he was content to purchase it by the sacrifice of reason, propriety and truth. A quibble was to him the fatal Cleopatra for which he lost the world, and was content to lose it."

William Wordsworth (1770–1850)

From *Miscellaneous Sonnets*, Part I, xxx, "It is a beauteous evening" (1807): "We must be free or die, who speak the tongue / That Shakespeare spake, the faith and morals hold / Which Milton held."

Ibid., i (1827): "Scorn not the sonnet. Critic, you have frowned, / Mindless of its just honours. With this key / Shakespeare unlocked his heart." (But cf. R. Browning, *House* [1876]: " 'With this same key / Shakespeare unlocked his heart' once more! / Did Shakespeare? If so, the less Shakespeare he!")

Samuel Taylor Coleridge (1772–1834)

From *Biographia Literaria* (1817): "Shakespeare, no mere child of Nature, no automaton of genius, no passive vehicle of inspiration possessed by the spirit, not possessing it, first studied patiently, meditated deeply, understood minutely, till knowledge, become habitual and intuitive, wedded itself to his habitual feelings and at length gave birth to that stupendous power by which he stands alone, with no equal or second in his own class."

Ibid.: "Our myriad-minded Shakespeare. . . . No man was ever yet a great poet, without being at the same time a profound philosopher."

From *Lectures* (publ. 1883): "I am deeply convinced that no man, however wide his erudition, however patient his antiquarian researches, can possibly understand, or be worthy of understanding, the writings of Shakespeare."

From *Table-Talk* (March 1834): "I believe Shakespeare was not a whit more intelligible in his own day than he is now to an educated man, except for a few local allusions of no consequence. He is of no age—nor of any religion, or party, or profession. The body and substance of his works came out of the unfathomable depths of his own oceanic mind. His observation and reading, which was considerable, supplied him with the drapery of his figures."

Thomas de Quincey (1785–1859)

From the essay "On the Knocking at the Gate in *Macbeth*" (1823): "From my boyish days I had always felt a great perplexity on one point in *Macbeth*. It was this. The knocking at the gate, which succeeds the murder of Duncan, produced to my feelings an effect for which I could never account. The effect was that it reflected back upon the murderer a peculiar awfulness and a depth of solemnity. Yet however obstinately I endeavoured with my understanding to comprehend this, for many years I could never see why it should produce such an effect."

John Keats (1795–1821)

From *Letters* (1817–20): "It struck me what quality went to form a man of achievement, especially in literature, and which Shakespeare possessed so enormously. I mean negative capability, that is, when a man is capable of being in uncertainties, mysteries and doubts, without any irritable reaching after fact and reason."

Ibid.: "Shakespeare led a life of allegory. His works are the comment on it."

Thomas Carlyle (1795–1881)

From *Heroes and Hero-Worship*, lecture III, "The Hero as Poet" (1840): "Whoever looks intelligently at this Shakespeare may recognize that he too was a prophet, in his way, of an insight analogous to the prophetic, though he took it up in another strain. Nature seemed to this man also divine, unspeakable, deep as Tophet, high as Heaven. . . . We called Dante the melodious priest of Middle-Age Catholicism. May we not call Shakespeare the still more melodious priest of a true Catholicism, the Universal Church of the future and of all times?"

Ibid.: "Indian Empire, or no Indian Empire, we cannot do without Shakespeare. Indian Empire will go, at any rate, some day. But this Shakespeare does not go, he lasts forever with us. We cannot give up our Shakespeare! . . . Yes, this Shakespeare is ours, we produced him, we speak and think by him, we are of one blood and kind with him."

John Henry Newman (1801–90)

From *The Idea of a University* (1873): "There surely is in all of us a cause for thankfulness that the most illustrious amongst English writers has so little of a Protestant about him that Catholics have been able without extravagance to claim him as their own, and that enemies to our creed have allowed that he is only not a Catholic because, and as far as, his times forbade it. . . . There is in Shakespeare neither contempt of religion nor skepticism, and he upholds the broad laws of moral and divine truth."

■ Matthew Arnold (1822–88)

From the sonnet "Shakespeare" (1849): "Others abide our question. Thou art free. / We ask and ask—thou smilest and art still, / Out-topping knowledge."

■ Gerard Manley Hopkins (1844–89)

From *Letters*, to Baillie (1864): "Shakespeare is and must be utterly the greatest of poets." To Dixon (1881): "After all it is the breadth of his human nature that we admire in Shakespeare." To Dixon (1883): "I think Shakespeare's drama is more in this sense romantic than the Greek, and that if unity of action is not so marked (as it is not) the interest of *romance*, arising from a well-calculated strain of incidents, is greater."

■ George Bernard Shaw (1856–1950)

From *Dramatic Opinions* (1907): "With the single exception of Homer, there is no eminent writer, not even Sir Walter Scott, whom I can despise so entirely as I despise Shakespeare when I measure my mind against his. . . . It would positively be a relief to me to dig him up and throw stones at him."

From *The Sanity of Art* (1908): "The writer who aims at producing the platitudes which are 'not for an age but for all time' has his reward in being unreadable in all ages, whilst Plato and Aristophanes trying to knock some sense into the Athens of their day, [and] Shakespeare peopling that same Athens with Elizabethan mechanics and Warwickshire hunts . . . are still alive and at home everywhere among the dust and ashes of many thousands of academic, punctilious, most archaeologically correct men of letters and art who spent their lives haughtily avoiding the journalist's vulgar obsession with the ephemeral."

Gilbert Keith Chesterton (1874–1936)

From *Chaucer* (1932): "That Shakespeare was a Catholic is a thing that every Catholic feels by every sort of convergent common sense to be true. It is supported by the few external and political facts we know, it is utterly unmistakable in the general spirit and atmosphere."

Ibid.: "The Renaissance genius was never so much intellectually inspired as when he seemed to be intellectually intoxicated, and his very depression was an exaltation. It would be something to be able even to despair like one of Shakespeare's characters. A dying man might want to live, if he could go on producing such phrases as 'Absent thee from felicity awhile'. He might even continue to absent himself. A murderer might grow cheerful, if he were able to utter his misery in those words about life being a thing 'full of sound and fury, signifying nothing'."

From *A Handful of Authors* (1953), "The Heroines of Shakespeare": "In this one virtue (of purity), in this one sex (of woman), something heroic and holy, something in the highest sense of the word fabulous, was felt to reside. Man was natural, but woman was supernatural."

Thomas Stearns Eliot (1888–1965)

From the essay "Hamlet" (1919): "So far from being Shakespeare's masterpiece, the play is most certainly an artistic failure. . . . *Coriolanus* may not be as 'interesting' as *Hamlet*, but it is, with *Antony and Cleopatra*, Shakespeare's most assured artistic success. And probably more people have thought *Hamlet* a work of art because they found it interesting, than have found it interesting because it is a work of art. It is the 'Mona Lisa' of literature."

Ibid.: "The only way of expressing emotion in the form of art is by finding an 'objective correlative'—in other words, a set of objects, a situation, a chain of events which shall be the formula of that *particular* emotion, such that when the external facts, which must terminate in sensory experience, are given, the emotion is immediately evoked."

From the essay "Dante" (1929): "There is an opacity, or inspissation of poetic style throughout Europe after the Renaissance."

Ibid.: "We do not understand Shakespeare from a single reading, and certainly not from a single play. There is a relation between the various plays of Shakespeare, taken in order. And it is a work of years to venture even one individual interpretation of the pattern in Shakespeare's carpet. . . . It is not certain that Shakespeare himself knew what it was."

Graham Greene (1904–91)

From the introduction to *The Autobiography of a Hunted Priest*, by John Gerard (1952): "Isn't there one whole area of the Elizabethan scene that we miss in Shakespeare's huge world of comedy and despair? The kings speak, the adventurers speak . . . the madmen and the lovers, the soldiers and the poets, but the martyrs are quite silent."

appendix 2
A Bibliography
on Shakespeare
and Christianity

Books Based on Groupings of Shakespeare's Plays

THE "FOUR GREAT TRAGEDIES" were famously dealt
with as a group by A. C. Bradley in his authoritative *Shakespearean Tragedy* (1904), but already the four "problem plays"
had been discussed by F. R. Boas in his *Shakespeare and His
Predecessors* (1896). Later on, E. M. W. Tillyard published
three such books: *Shakespeare's History Plays* (1944), with the
division of the dramatist's material into two main tetralogies
covering the history of England from the reign of Richard II
to that of Richard III; *Shakespeare's Problem Plays* (1971), following the same selection as that made by Boas; and *Shakespeare's Last Plays* (1938), dealing chiefly with *Cymbeline, The
Winter's Tale*, and *The Tempest*. A better grouping for the last
plays, which should at least include *Pericles*, is that proposed
by R. G. Hunter in his *Shakespeare and the Comedy of For-
giveness* (1965). Here, to my shame, I have to confess I have
followed most of these groupings in my first book on Shakespeare, *An Introduction to Shakespeare's Plays* (1964).

Christian Interpretations of Shakespeare's Plays
Among the many such books on the Christian interpreta-
tions of Shakespeare's plays that came out after World War II,

I may begin with George Wilson Knight's *The Crown of Life* (1947) on the final plays; then John Danby's *Shakespeare's Doctrine of Nature* (1949), especially the section on *King Lear*; M. D. Parker's fine study *The Slave of Life* (1955); Paul Siegel's *Shakespearean Tragedy and the Elizabethan Compromise* (1957); John Vyvyan's *The Shakespearian Ethic* (1959); Maynard Mack's *King Lear in Our Time* (1965); and notably Roy Battenhouse's *Shakespearean Tragedy, Its Art and Its Christian Premises* (1969), followed by his later anthology of *Shakespeare's Christian Dimension* (1993), including a contribution of mine on *King Lear*.

The Christian approach to Shakespeare's plays, however, suffered an ironical setback with the publication of Roland Frye's *Shakespeare and Christian Doctrine* (1963), justifying a purely secular approach from the viewpoint of three major Reformation theologians, Luther, Calvin, and Hooker, and specifically attacking what he termed "the School of Knight." His book was shortly followed by W. R. Elton's *King Lear and the Gods* (1965), proposing an agnostic approach to this dramatic masterpiece, with abundant documentation from contemporary writings. From then onward the secular approach became the "orthodoxy" of the Shakespeare "establishment," now beginning to organize itself worldwide, and coming to a climax in Samuel Schoenbaum's *William Shakespeare: A Documentary Life* (1975).

Shakespeare and the Bible

For books on Shakespeare's use of the Bible, we have to go back to the Victorian bishop Charles Wordsworth (the poet William Wordsworth's nephew) with his *Shakespeare's Knowledge and Use of the Bible* (1864), to Thomas Carter's *Shakespeare and Holy Scripture* (1905), and to the more authoritative Richmond Noble's *Shakespeare's Biblical Knowledge*

(1935). Partly relying on these three books, I published my own study, *Biblical Themes in Shakespeare* (1975), before going on to make a more special study, *Biblical Influence in the Great Tragedies* (1985), which was republished in America in 1986 under the altered title of *Biblical Influences in Shakespeare's Great Tragedies*. At the same time, Naseeb Shaheen in America brought out his *Biblical References in Shakespeare's Tragedies* (1987), following it up with *Shakespeare's History Plays* (1989) and *Shakespeare's Comedies* (1993). Of all these books I may claim that mine alone bring out the impact of biblical influence on the thematic meaning of the plays.

Shakespeare and Catholicism

The special study of Shakespeare's Catholic allegiance goes back to the Victorian scholar-friend of Newman, Richard Simpson, whose notes on the subject were used by a priest of the Oratory, Henry Bowden, in his book *The Religion of Shakespeare* (1899). A more general survey of the poet's religious formation was undertaken by John Henry de Groot, a Protestant minister, in *The Shakespeares and 'The Old Faith'* (1946), and a more thorough study of the poet's religion in relation to his friends and acquaintances was produced by two German scholars, Heinrich Mutschmann and Karl Wentersdorf, and was translated into English as *Shakespeare and Catholicism* (1952). Here I came into the field with my wider study, *Shakespeare's Religious Background* (1973), considering the extent to which the various religious influences of the dramatist's age, Catholic, Protestant, Puritan, and even atheistic, have entered into the plays while concluding that on balance the Catholic element is the strongest. This book I subsequently followed up with two bibliographical studies: *The Religious Controversies of the Elizabethan Age* (1977) and

Religious Controversies of the Jacobean Age (1978). My interpretation was subsequently supported by Ian Wilson in his
biographical survey *Shakespeare, the Evidence* (1993), the only
biography of Shakespeare written from a Catholic viewpoint.
I then came out more into the open with two books proposing a Catholic interpretation of the plays, *The Catholicism of
Shakespeare's Plays* (1997) and *Shakespeare's Apocalypse* (2000),
the latter on the four tragedies. In the same year Carol Enos,
though not herself a Catholic, published her book *Shakespeare and the Catholic Religion*. More recently I have devoted
two books to the related subject of "metadrama," as seen in
detail in Shakespeare's great tragedies: *Shakespeare's Metadrama: Hamlet and Macbeth* (2003) and *Shakespeare's Metadrama: Othello and King Lear* (2004). Then there is my latest
book, *Shakespeare the Papist* (2005), which came out simulta-
neously and coincidentally with Clare Asquith's *Shadowplay*.

Shakespeare's Catholic Formation
and the Shakeshafte Theory

Over the past few decades a certain theory has come to the
fore applying the old tradition, that the young Shakespeare
had been "a schoolmaster in the country," to a certain gifted
young tutor-player whose name had been found mentioned
in a will, dated 1581, of a Catholic gentleman in Lancashire,
Alexander Houghton of Lea Hall near Preston. The theory
was seemingly refuted by the criticism of Schoenbaum in his
authoritative biography, but it was subsequently revived by
E. A. J. Honigmann with answering scholarship in his metic-
ulous study *Shakespeare, The "Lost Years"* (1986)—incidentally supporting my arguments in favor of the theory against
Schoenbaum's rebuttal of them. Honigmann's work paved
the way for an important conference held at the University
of Lancaster in 1999 entitled "Lancastrian Shakespeare,"

which practically meant "Shakespeare's Catholic Back-ground," since only a reliable Catholic would have been trusted as tutor and player in such a Catholic household. The proceedings of this conference have at last been published under the title of *Lancastrian Shakespeare* (2003) in two volumes, including my essay, "Shakespeare's Jesuit Schoolmasters," considering how many of the masters at the Stratford Grammar School were connected both with the Jesuits and with Lancashire. Interestingly, the following year another conference, "Shakespeare and Religions," was held at Stratford, and the proceedings were published in a subsequent issue of *The Shakespeare Survey* (2001), including another contribution of mine, "Religion in Arden." Yet another of my essays, based on the probable meeting of Shakespeare and Campion in Lancashire, came out as a monograph titled *The Plays and the Exercises: A Hidden Source of Shakespeare's Inspiration?* (2002). Subsequently, there appeared an anthology of essays by American scholars on the same subject under the title *Shakespeare and the Culture of Christianity in Early Modern England* (2003), which was dedicated to me as a pioneer in this field. Today it is still a very live subject, all the more as it has for so long been suppressed, under a kind of taboo by "orthodox" scholars, as belonging to the "lunatic fringe" of Shakespeare studies.

Subject Index

See also *Character Index* for references
to *dramatis personae* in plays

Character Index

Characters are listed under surname or first name rather than title (Lady Anne is under A, Friar Laurence under L, Don John under J). Characters known only by a noble title are listed under the main element (Arragon, Prince of; Hastings). See also *Subject Index*, for characters who are also real persons

Achilles *(Troilus and Cressida)*, 108, 109, 114

Adriana *(Comedy of Errors)*, 28

Aegeon *(Comedy of Errors)*, 28

Aemilia *(Comedy of Errors)*, 28

Agamemnon *(Troilus and Cressida)*, 108

Aguecheek, Sir Andrew *(Twelfth Night)*, 92, 93, 110

Lady Anne *(Richard III)*, 21

Antipholus of Ephesus *(Comedy of Errors)*, 28

Antipholus of Syracuse *(Comedy of Errors)*, 28

Antonio *(Merchant of Venice)*, 30, 58–63, 98

Antonio *(Two Gentlemen of Verona)*, 31

Antony
(Antony and Cleopatra), 114
(Julius Caesar), 79–81, 108

Arragon, Prince of *(Merchant of Venice)*, 60

Arthur *(King John)*, 46

Audrey *(As You Like It)*, 70

Autolycus *(Winter's Tale)*, 83

Bassanio *(Merchant of Venice)*, 30, 37, 58–64

Bassianus *(Titus Andronicus)*, 36

Beatrice *(Much Ado About Nothing)*, 86–89

Belch, Sir Toby *(Twelfth Night)*, 92, 93, 94

Benedick *(Much Ado About Nothing)*, 86–89

Berowne *(Love's Labour's Lost)*, 33